M000087751

Marriage Makers
Marriage Breakers

Dr. Bo Wagner

Word of His Mouth Publishers
Mooresboro, NC

All Scripture quotations are taken from the **King James Version** of the Bible.

ISBN: 978-1-941039-90-8
Printed in the United States of America
© 2014 Dr. Bo Wagner (Robert Arthur Wagner)

Word of His Mouth Publishers
Mooresboro, NC
www.wordofhismouth.com

Cover Art: Chip Nuhrah

All rights reserved. No part of this publication may be reproduced in any form without the prior written permission of the publisher except for quotations in printed reviews.

Table of Content Page

4

Introduction

Song of Solomon 2:16a *My beloved is mine, and I am his...*

There is a reason I begin with this text. Why? Because it is the ideal that we should be striving for in our marriage! The couple in the Song of Solomon were wildly, passionately in love with each other. They spoke of each other in terms that would make most people blush. Even a king could not break them up. They were marriage makers, and they made a good one.

A great many people in the Bible were marriage makers. They did what was necessary to produce a marriage relationship that would stand the test of time and trials.

But there were others in the Bible who were marriage breakers. They could have had a wonderful marriage relationship, but they were unwilling to do so. Instead, they did the things necessary to destroy a home.

A home can be either heaven on earth or hell on earth, and either result is the predictable outcome of how a husband and wife behave toward each other. The good news is that the Word of God, the Bible, gives us many, many examples both of what to do and of what not to do! A husband and wife who study these marriages found in

Scripture can find everything they need to know to be a marriage maker rather than a marriage breaker.

And that is the purpose of this book. Eighteen couples from Scripture are found within these pages. Some were marriage makers, some were marriage breakers. All of them have a story to tell, a story you should pay close attention to. May your marriage be saved, sweetened, and strengthened through this book.

Chapter 1
The Proverbs 31 Man

"Greetings and salutations!

"I am honored to be allowed to communicate with you by letter and to tell you of my experience as a husband. Truthfully, I do not blame you if you have never heard of me, nor do I mind. I am no one important; I just happen to have been married to the greatest wife ever.

"Men, I do not mean to make you jealous, but my wife was the greatest thing since Eve herself. For starters, she was very easy on the eyes. Do you think me unspiritual for starting there? That is entirely up to you, but I personally enjoy being able to rejoice in having a beautiful spouse! My wife's looks were not by accident. She was physically fit. She worked out; she was strong.

"But that does not begin to tell the whole story of this wonderful woman. She was smart, oh so very smart! I often bored of talking to other men, longing only to get home and speak to my wife. She could converse intelligently on so many subjects yet was never proud. In fact, she was always kind.

"May I tell you something? I really did have it all as a husband! This woman could cook, clean, work, talk, invest, and do it all with grace and charm. She actually made me famous! I ended up being known as 'her husband' rather than her being known as my wife! Who am I? Why, I am the Proverbs 31 Man."

Every preacher has likely preached message after message on the Proverbs 31 woman. Tens of thousands of books have been written about the Proverbs 31 woman. But this great woman had a great husband, and it is time we give him his due! Let us examine the text and see what we can learn from this marriage maker.

Proverbs 31:10 *Who can find a virtuous woman? for her price is far above rubies.* **11** *The heart of **her husband** doth safely trust in her, so that **he** shall have no need of spoil.* **12** *She will do **him** good and not evil all the days of her life.* **13** *She seeketh wool, and flax, and worketh willingly with her hands.* **14** *She is like the merchants' ships; she bringeth her food from afar.* **15** *She riseth also while it is yet night, and giveth meat to her household, and a portion to her maidens.* **16** *She considereth a field, and buyeth it: with the fruit of her hands she planteth a vineyard.* **17** *She girdeth her loins with strength, and strengtheneth her arms.* **18** *She perceiveth that her merchandise is good: her candle goeth not out by night.* **19** *She layeth her hands to the spindle, and her hands hold the distaff.* **20** *She stretcheth out her hand to the poor; yea, she reacheth forth her hands to the needy.* **21** *She is not afraid of the snow for her household: for all her household are clothed with scarlet.* **22** *She maketh herself coverings of tapestry; her clothing is silk and purple.* **23** ***Her husband** is known in the gates, when **he** sitteth among the elders of the land.* **24** *She maketh fine linen, and selleth it; and delivereth girdles unto the merchant.* **25** *Strength and honour are her clothing; and she shall rejoice in time to come.* **26** *She openeth her mouth with wisdom; and in her tongue is the law of kindness.* **27** *She looketh well to the ways of her household, and eateth not the bread of idleness.* **28**

*Her children arise up, and call her blessed; **her husband** also, and he praiseth her.* **29** *Many daughters have done virtuously, but thou excellest them all.* **30** *Favour is deceitful, and beauty is vain: but a woman that feareth the LORD, she shall be praised.* **31** *Give her of the fruit of her hands; and let her own works praise her in the gates.*

No less than six times in this passage the Proverbs 31 man is mentioned, and he is mentioned by implication many more times than that. This was a great woman, but she was a great woman with a great and wise husband, and there is a ton that we can learn from him! So let's jump in.

This was a husband that determined to find everything he needed to find in his wife

Proverbs 31:11 *The heart of her husband doth safely trust in her, so that he shall have no need of spoil.*

That last phrase *so that he shall have no need of spoil* is a very telling one. It indicates that this man, this husband, had determined to find everything he needed to find, in his wife rather than somewhere else. Now, yes, she was obviously amazing. But please believe me when I as a marriage counselor of two decades or more tell you that the one can actually produce the other. In other words, when a man is smart enough to be "all in" with his wife, she will very likely respond by becoming exactly what he needs anyway!

Husbands, you have awesome power to make your wife what you wish that she was! A wife responds to a "no reservations" kind of husband.

Say that out loud, please, "A wife responds to a 'no reservations' kind of husband."

Sir, when you got married, you made a "no reservations" kind of commitment. Fulfilling that commitment makes a wife into something very special. They are designed by God to respond to that.

9

If you will spend your time telling your wife that she is the prettiest person you know, she will believe it, and she will become it. She will start to glow with a confidence that makes her incredibly beautiful.

If you will spend your time cultivating a relationship with your wife to the exclusion of all other women, she will respond and become the best friend that you have in this world.

The Proverbs 31 man was "all in" with his wife, there were no chips left on the table to play anywhere else. Believe me on this, if you have hesitancy or reservation in your heart toward your wife, she will sense it, and it will cause problems. But if you abandon yourself to your wife, she will sense that too, and she will become something truly amazing.

This was a husband who encouraged his wife to show initiative and to be creative

Proverbs 31:13 *She seeketh wool, and flax, and worketh willingly with her hands.* **14** *She is like the merchants' ships; she bringeth her food from afar.*

None of this was possible in those days without a husband's encouragement. And men back then most definitely did not encourage it! This woman was importing exotic foods to feed her family; she was out and about exploring and finding wool and flax. She had been unshackled by her husband, and the result was a creative dynamo!

Sir, do not be afraid of your wife.

And as I write those words, I can almost hear the visceral reaction that is sure to come from some quarters:

"Whut? I ain't afeared o no blessed woe-man!"

Uh, beg to differ with you there, Cletus, but you are exactly the kind of man that is afraid of a woman. You are afraid that she will think that she can do better than you, so

10

you spend all of your time berating her and belittling her and bringing her down. You figure that if you can tear her down far enough, she will never have the confidence to leave. Basically, your problem is...you're stupid.

The smartest thing a husband can ever do is unshackle his wife and release her creativity and encourage her to dream and to do. A wife is going to respond to that, and you will be glad of how she responds!

This was a husband who allowed his wife to use her brain
Proverbs 31:16 *She considereth a field, and buyeth it: with the fruit of her hands she planteth a vineyard.*

This amazing woman had an amazing husband who allowed his amazing wife to have and use a brain. It does not say that "they" considered a field, it does not say that "he" considered a field, it says that "she" considered a field and bought it. She used her brain to figure out whether or not something was a good deal and she acted on it.

Sir, your wife came complete with a lot of body parts that you really enjoy, but if you are smart, you will learn to enjoy her brain as much as anything else.

I am always amazed at how smart some very dumb men think they are. They think they are smart, but they are dumb enough to treat their wives like they are dumb, and even to try and keep them dumb.

Sir, if you are one of those idiot ogres, I feel sorry for you.

A church a couple of hours from mine hired a youth pastor. The church took a trip somewhere, and the pastor's wife came up to him and said, "Brother so and so, let's put the guys up in your bus and the girls back here with me." A perfectly reasonable and wise suggestion.

The punk stuck his finger in her face and said, "Stay in your place, woman. I'll handle this!"

11

Now, for starters, please be aware that if anything like that ever happens at my church, if she does not do you great bodily harm, I will.

Secondly, can you imagine being married to a horse's rear end like that? How miserable must his wife be! Sir, God gave your wife a brain, and you will be a wise man the day you learn to let her use it.

What has happened at our church, going from nothing to an amazing work in a fairly short period of time, has happened at least partly because I have utilized my wife's brain so very many times! She is brilliant, and I am blessed because of it!

This was a husband who allowed his wife to be physically fit

Proverbs 31:17 *She girdeth her loins with strength, and strengtheneth her arms.*

This woman had fit, strong, shapely arms and legs.

I can almost hear the men at this point saying, "Well who in the world would ever have a problem with that?" Apparently, more husbands than you may realize. It seems that every man says they want a fit, strong wife, but when it comes down to the actual doing, then the story changes.

"I want a fit, strong wife! I don't want her to ever be out of the kitchen, but I want a fit, strong wife."

"I want a fit, strong wife! I'm gonna make sure she cleans house all day every day, but I want a fit, strong wife."

"I want a fit, strong wife! I ain't buyin' no exercise equipment since I need a new huntin' rifle, but I want a fit, strong wife."

"I want a fit, strong wife! I ain't gonna exercise with her, cause a guy looks good with a big ol' gut floppin' over his belt, but I want a fit, strong wife."

"I want a fit, strong wife! She ain't goin' to no gym, but I want a fit, strong wife."

Excuse me sir, it really does not sound much like you want a fit, strong wife at all! And by the way, preachers are some of the biggest hypocrites in the world about this. They will spend two hours a day at a gym, staring at all the fit little things in their leotards, but will not let their wife go, and then complain that she is out of shape. You sorry sack of horse snot.

This man, the Proverbs 31 man, allowed his wife to be physically fit.

This was a husband who had built up his wife's confidence

Proverbs 31:18 *She perceiveth that her merchandise is good: her candle goeth not out by night.*

I really like this verse and the implications of it. How do you think this woman realized that her merchandise was good? I will tell you how it did not happen; it did not happen by him tearing it and her down all the time. This was clearly a man who spent his time building up his wife's confidence. Men, if you spend time building up your wife's confidence, you will produce a tiger instead of a tabby cat!

I have tried very hard to build up my wife's confidence since the day I met her. I realized I was doing a pretty good job the day she took Bluto down to size. We used to have a man at our church that looked just like Bluto from the old Popeye cartoons: four hundred fifty pounds, scraggly beard, booming voice, and had been in the Navy. He berated and belittled and bullied his own wife and kid constantly and always got his way by doing so. One day he walked into my wife's office, slapped a stack of papers down on her desk and said, "Here, make copies of these!" She picked them up and slapped them right back at him and said, "Do it yourself!"

That is exactly the kind of confident woman I want! A confident woman is a ROWWWWWWWRR kind of woman!

This was a husband who allowed and encouraged his wife to be tender hearted

Proverbs 31:20 *She stretcheth out her hand to the poor; yea, she reacheth forth her hands to the needy.*

This was a lifestyle for this woman, and as such, would have had to be encouraged by her husband. She was generous, merciful, tender-hearted, and desirous to meet the needs of others.

Sir, God made the wife, by nature, to be the more tender-hearted of the two. You need to feed that and encourage it.

May I teach you something? If you squelch that tender-heartedness in her, you may one day live long enough to regret it. I do not think I would want to be the old man in a nursing home who had spent years making sure that his wife was not tender-hearted toward the hurting and needy.

If she wants to volunteer, let her. If she wants to make someone a meal, let her. If she wants to adopt an orphan, let her. The Proverbs 31 man was smart enough to do so, and it did not hurt him a bit.

This was a husband who allowed his wife to dress well

Proverbs 31:22 *She maketh herself coverings of tapestry; her clothing is silk and purple.*

Yes, she made these clothes, but Mr. Breadwinner had to do his job to get the material and then had to allow the making thereof. If there had been a Belks or Dillards or whatever in those days, I can guarantee you that Mr. 31 would have no doubt let her go shopping.

They say that clothes make the man. I kind of doubt that. But I do not doubt for a second that clothes make the woman. I have studied my wife through the years, and I have found something out. The days when she can dress sharp and look amazing, she actually feels better about herself. That is going to be true of most every woman.

Sir, you would be better off without the new gun if it means getting your wife a new dress.

Sir, you better budget for nice clothes for your wife. If she feels confident and pretty all during the day, you are likely to feel very happy later. As I say so often in my old Indian voice:

Treat woman right, when sun in sky, she treat you right, when moon up high...

This was a husband who made something of himself, so that his wife could have a husband to be proud of

Proverbs 31:23 *Her husband is known in the gates, when he sitteth among the elders of the land.*

Sir, when a woman gets married, she is very largely tying her fate to you. She changes her name to yours. She trusts you as a provider. Her reputation becomes tied to yours. If you stagnate and become a lump on the couch, she will suffer for it! But if you have enough character to work and plan and invest and work some more and dream and do and build and work and create and work...

You are the water level that will either lift your wife or lower your wife. Sir, make something of yourself! Do not doom your wife to a life of dependency upon government. Do not doom your wife to a life of boredom. Do not doom your wife to a life of living in a tiny rental trailer and watching the bug zapper each night for entertainment. Make something of yourself, and your wife will benefit for it!

This was a husband who knew the power of praise

Proverbs 31:28 *Her children arise up, and call her blessed; her husband also, and he praiseth her.*

I believe God very clearly saved the best for last in all of this. There is nothing, nothing so powerful as verbal praise. Think of how God Himself feels about it.

Psalm 107:8 *Oh that men would praise the LORD for his goodness, and for his wonderful works to the children of men!*

Psalm 107:15 *Oh that men would praise the LORD for his goodness, and for his wonderful works to the children of men!*

Psalm 107:21 *Oh that men would praise the LORD for his goodness, and for his wonderful works to the children of men!*

Psalm 107:31 *Oh that men would praise the LORD for his goodness, and for his wonderful works to the children of men!*

Why should a woman feel any different?

You can say, "He praised her because of what she was," if you want to, but you will never convince me that he did not start praising her until the very end of the story! If he had not been praising her the whole time, she would never have become this successful to begin with!

There is awesome power in praise. I have never once known a woman to become an awesome wife by being berated into it, but I have known plenty that became awesome wives by being praised into it.

Here is a letter I came across a few years ago, I apologize that I do not know the source. I just know it is very, very good!

Larry and Jo Ann were an ordinary couple. They lived in an ordinary house on an ordinary street. They struggled to make

16

ends meet and to do the right things for their children. They were ordinary in yet another way...they had their squabbles. Much of their conversation concerned what was wrong in their marriage and who was to blame. Until one day when a most extraordinary event took place.

"You know, Jo Ann, I've got a magic chest of drawers. Every time I open them, they're full of socks and underwear," Larry said. "I want to thank you for filling them all these years."

Jo Ann stared at her husband over the top of her glasses. "What do you want, Larry?"

"I just want you to know I appreciate those magic drawers."

Jo Ann pushed the incident out of her mind until a few days later.

"Jo Ann, thank you for recording so many correct check numbers in the ledger this month. You put down the right numbers fifteen out of sixteen times. That's a record."

Disbelieving what she had heard, Jo Ann looked up from her mending. "Larry, you're always complaining about my recording the wrong check numbers. Why stop now?"

"No reason, I just wanted to let you know I appreciate the effort."

Jo Ann shook her head and went back to her mending. "What's gotten into him?" she thought. She tried to disregard it, but Larry's strange behavior intensified.

"Jo Ann, that was a great dinner," he said one evening. "I appreciate all your effort. Why in the past fifteen years I'll bet you've fixed over 14,000 meals for me and the kids."

Then, "Jo Ann, the house looks spiffy." And even "Thanks, Jo Ann, just for being you. I really enjoy your company."

Jo Ann was growing worried. Where's the sarcasm, the criticism?

But Jo Ann's step was now a little lighter.

That would be the end of the story except one day another extraordinary event took place. This time it was Jo Ann who spoke. "Larry," she said, "I want to thank you for going to work and providing for us all these years. I don't think I've ever told you how much I appreciate it."

Larry never revealed the reason for his dramatic change of behavior...but it's one I'm thankful to live with. You see, I am Jo Ann.

Her husband praiseth her...

Chapter 2
The Smartest Husband in the World

The second letter we shall read is from the Don Juan of marriage; the man who knew how to make a woman fall in love with him.

"Greetings and salutations!

"It is my joy to correspond with you this evening. I was no one special by the standards of this world. I was a shepherd and a vine tender. But to one woman, my wife, I was greater than Solomon himself!

"Men, as I observe how things are done in the 21st century, may I kindly make an observation? Many husbands know about as much about romance as politicians do about spending money wisely.

"Where has the fire gone? The romance? The passion? The beautiful insanity that is marital romantic love? Men, marriage is not nearly as complicated as some of you make it out to be. Your job is to make your wife fall madly in love with you, every day for the rest of your life.

"What is that, you say? It cannot be done? Au contraire, friend, it can. I did it. Pay attention, and you can do the same. What are my qualifications to make such a bold statement, you ask? Who am I? I am the romantic; I am the groom of the Song of Solomon."

Song of Solomon 1:1 *The song of songs, which is Solomon's. 2 Let him kiss me with the kisses of his mouth: for thy love is better than wine. 3 Because of the savour of thy good ointments thy name is as ointment poured forth, therefore do the virgins love thee. 4 Draw me, we will run after thee: the king hath brought me into his chambers: we will be glad and rejoice in thee, we will remember thy love more than wine: the upright love thee. 5 I am black, but comely, O ye daughters of Jerusalem, as the tents of Kedar, as the curtains of Solomon. 6 Look not upon me, because I am black, because the sun hath looked upon me: my mother's children were angry with me; they made me the keeper of the vineyards; but mine own vineyard have I not kept. 7 Tell me, O thou whom my soul loveth, where thou feedest, where thou makest thy flock to rest at noon: for why should I be as one that turneth aside by the flocks of thy companions? 8 If thou know not, O thou fairest among women, go thy way forth by the footsteps of the flock, and feed thy kids beside the shepherds' tents. 9 I have compared thee, O my love, to a company of horses in Pharaoh's chariots. 10 Thy cheeks are comely with rows of jewels, thy neck with chains of gold. 11 We will make thee borders of gold with studs of silver. 12 While the king sitteth at his table, my spikenard sendeth forth the smell thereof. 13 A bundle of myrrh is my well beloved unto me; he shall lie all night betwixt my breasts. 14 My beloved is unto me as a cluster of camphire in the vineyards of Engedi. 15 Behold, thou art fair, my love; behold, thou art fair; thou hast doves' eyes. 16 Behold, thou art fair, my beloved, yea, pleasant: also our bed is green. 17 The beams of our house are cedar, and our rafters of fir.*

There are some really dumb men out there who end up becoming really dumb husbands or really dumb would-be husbands. The husband in the Song of Solomon was not like this. He is the man I like to call "the smartest husband in the world." Let's work our way through this passage and see what there is to see.

The hopelessly devoted bride

    Song of Solomon 1:2 *Let him kiss me with the kisses of his mouth: for thy love is better than wine.* **3** *Because of the savour of thy good ointments thy name is as ointment poured forth, therefore do the virgins love thee.* **4** *Draw me, we will run after thee: the king hath brought me into his chambers: we will be glad and rejoice in thee, we will remember thy love more than wine: the upright love thee.*

    The verses above introduce the bride of the book to us. The first thing we learn about her is how she feels about the man she is going to write about. It is very clear that she is utterly smitten with him!

    Moving ahead to verses twelve through fourteen, we will see how she began to feel about him early on in their marriage, and it was all good.

    Song of Solomon 1:12 *While the king sitteth at his table, my spikenard sendeth forth the smell thereof.* **13** *A bundle of myrrh is my wellbeloved unto me; he shall lie all night betwixt my breasts.* **14** *My beloved is unto me as a cluster of camphire in the vineyards of Engedi.*

    The rest of the book shows this lady to be hopelessly, madly in love with her husband. Even a king could not pry her away! Listen to just a sampling of what she says about him in this book:

    Song of Solomon 1:16a *Behold, thou art fair, my beloved, yea, pleasant...*

    (You look so good; you are a delight to me!)

    Song of Solomon 2:3 *As the apple tree among the trees of the wood, so is my beloved among the sons. I sat* *down under his shadow with great delight, and his fruit was sweet to my taste.*

(Other guys may qualify as pine trees, or kudzu, or little shrubs, but you are an apple tree, baby...)

Song of Solomon 2:8 *The voice of my beloved! behold, he cometh leaping upon the mountains, skipping upon the hills.*

(I can hear him! I can't see him yet, but I can hear him. Man, I can't wait till he is here...)

Song of Solomon 2:9 *My beloved is like a roe or a young hart: behold, he standeth behind our wall, he looketh forth at the windows, shewing himself through the lattice.*

(My man is young and in shape, and whoo! He is showing me some of that shape...I like it!)

Song of Solomon 2:16 *My beloved is mine, and I am his: he feedeth among the lilies.*

(We are the only people on earth for each other...)

Song of Solomon 4:16 *Awake, O north wind; and come, thou south; blow upon my garden, that the spices thereof may flow out. Let my beloved come into his garden, and eat his pleasant fruits.*

(This is your invitation, big boy. Just consider me your own personal garden. I am waiting for you...)

Song of Solomon 5:10 *My beloved is white and ruddy, the chiefest among ten thousand.* **11** *His head is as the most fine gold, his locks are bushy, and black as a raven.* **12** *His eyes are as the eyes of doves by the rivers of waters, washed with milk, and fitly set.* **13** *His cheeks are as a bed of spices, as sweet flowers: his lips like lilies, dropping sweet smelling myrrh.* **14** *His hands are as gold rings set with the beryl: his belly is as bright ivory overlaid with sapphires.* **15** *His legs are as pillars of marble, set upon sockets of fine gold: his countenance is as Lebanon, excellent as the cedars.* **16** *His mouth is most sweet: yea, he is altogether lovely. This* *is my beloved, and this is my friend, O daughters of Jerusalem.*

(My man looks goooooood!)

Song of Solomon 6:3 *I am my beloved's, and my beloved is mine: he feedeth among the lilies.*

(Did I mention that we are the only people on earth for each other?)

Song of Solomon 7:10 *I am my beloved's, and his desire is toward me.* **11** *Come, my beloved, let us go forth into the field; let us lodge in the villages.* **12** *Let us get up early to the vineyards; let us see if the vine flourish, whether the tender grape appear, and the pomegranates bud forth: there will I give thee my loves.* **13** *The mandrakes give a smell, and at our gates are all manner of pleasant fruits, new and old, which I have laid up for thee, O my beloved.*

(Let's travel together. I promise to make it worth your time!)

Song of Solomon 8:14 *Make haste, my beloved, and be thou like to a roe or to a young hart upon the mountains of spices.*

(I only have one last verse to say it. I love you, baby, please hurry home...)

This woman is hopelessly devoted to her man! And the whole key, the place where it all began, is back at the very beginning of this book. You see, a dumb man says, "I wish my woman was like that for me! If I had a woman that treated me like that, I could be a regular 'Don Ju-wan!'" No, doofus, a regular 'Don Ju-wan' will produce a woman like this! It was what the man did that made this woman hopelessly devoted. So let's go back to the first chapter and find out what this guy did.

The highly defensive bride

Song of Solomon 1:5 *I am black, but comely, O ye daughters of Jerusalem, as the tents of Kedar, as the curtains of Solomon.*

This woman, chapter six calls her the Shulamite, is not from Israel. Nor is she from the regions of Africa, as you might suspect from her description as black. The next verse lets us know that her skin has been darkened because she was forced to stay out in the sun all day.

There were other women there, girls who were from Jerusalem. They were not like this. Their skin was still fair and pretty, as far as they were concerned. They looked at this sunburned woman, they looked at her man, a man that they wanted also, and it does not take a rocket scientist to figure out what happened next. There was a cat fight. They gave this poor girl fits, they made fun of her dark skin, they called her names.

And look how she answered them. "I am black but comely! I am black, but I am beautiful. My skin is damaged, but I look better than you! So if you have anything else to say to me, just bring your botox-lipped, lipo-hipped, hair dye- dipped self on over here and let's git it on!"

Man, she is letting them have it! But do you know what? Nothing has changed for her yet. She is speaking her mind, but she has not been changed. She is defensive, but defensive will not do the job.

She may not have liked these girls, but she did have a problem. Even though the other girls were being snots to her, they were right in their estimation of her. And as long as she stayed there and argued with them, nothing would ever change.

The helplessly despondent bride

Song of Solomon 1:6 *Look not upon me, because I am black, because the sun hath looked upon me: my mother's* *children were angry with me; they made me the keeper of the vineyards; but mine own vineyard have I not kept.*

In this verse she is no longer speaking to the other women, she has moved into the presence of her man. The stinging words of those other girls are still ringing in her ears, and maybe there is a tear or two streaming down her face. Her husband is looking at her, and she is self-conscious. She bows her head and turns away a bit and says, "Don't look at me. I have a physical flaw. My skin is all damaged..."

And then she tells him what she did not tell the other girls. She tells him why she is like that. She tells him about what things were like back home.

This girl is broken. She is hurting inside because of what she is outside. She knows deep down that the other girls were right about her. Thank God this bride in the Song of Solomon finally went from highly defensive to helplessly despondent, because that then led her to the next necessary step.

The humbly desirous bride

Song of Solomon 1:7 *Tell me, O thou whom my soul loveth, where thou feedest, where thou makest thy flock to rest at noon: for why should I be as one that turneth aside by the flocks of thy companions?*

As she continues talking to her man, she stops thinking about herself and begins to focus on him. She may not like who she is, but she certainly likes who he is. She says, "I know you'll be taking a break at noon. Tell me where you are going to be. I want to come to you. From what the other girls said, I know I do not deserve you. I should probably focus on some other lesser guy...but if there is any chance I can have you, I want you! Why should I turn aside by the flocks of one of your companions if I can have you?"

25

She is hurting, she is scarred, she is scared, but she is willing to risk everything and open her heart up to her husband. That is a huge thing. And that is when the smartest husband in the world steps up and does his thing. Here is where he turns his wife into the hopelessly devoted bride.

Song of Solomon 1:8 *If thou know not, O thou fairest among women, go thy way forth by the footsteps of the flock, and feed thy kids beside the shepherds' tents.*

Get this picture in your mind: she comes before him, still damaged and flawed, sunburned, uncertain, insecure... and the first thing he calls her is *thou fairest among women*! In one master stroke he has taken her insecurities and erased them. If your wife knows that you see her like this, no other man on earth is likely to stand a chance with her.

The next thing he does is tell her where to find him so they can rendezvous...*go thy way forth by the footsteps of the flock, and feed thy kids beside the shepherds' tents.*

This was so that they could meet up and spend quality time together.

The next thing he does is describe how he sees her.

Song of Solomon 1:9 *I have compared thee, O my love, to a company of horses in Pharaoh's chariots.* **10** *Thy cheeks are comely with rows of jewels, thy neck with chains of gold.* **11** *We will make thee borders of gold with studs of silver.*

He positively waxed eloquent with her. This was a man that did not think poetry to be unmanly. This was a man that knew the power of the spoken word. "You are beautiful; you are worthy of all my best jewels..."

And do you know what is never a single time mentioned again in the rest of this book? Her skin damage is never mentioned again. He took this dear woman, tended to her and nourished her, erased every single one of her insecurities, and in so doing made her as beautiful as he already saw her.

A husband who makes it his life's mission to erase and remove every insecurity that his wife has, and even to transform those negatives into something that she views as positives, will have similar results.

The smartest husband in the world indeed!

Chapter 3
The Wife Who Made a Good Marriage
Out of a Bad One

"Greetings and salutations most noble assembly!

"I think it an honor to correspond with you in this manner. My marriage truly was a unique one, from the very first day till the very last day, and even beyond the very last day! May I first of all say that I would not recommend for you to start your marriage in the manner in which I started mine. My husband did not want to marry me. How did I change his mind? I did not. I tricked him into thinking I was someone else, specifically, my sister.

"Of course, that started our marriage off on a bit of the wrong foot. To make matters worse, my husband was a polygamist, and the other woman was my sister, the woman that he wanted to begin with!

"I was obviously not the perfect wife. But may I tell you one thing that I honestly can say? I loved my husband. He meant everything to me! I would rather have died than ever be without him.

"Most people would not have felt that way. My husband, God rest his soul, was 'honesty challenged.' I suppose that is a nice way of saying that he was a liar. He also hated me. And then there was the fact that he was not very manly. Truthfully, our marriage had everything going against it and almost nothing going for it, and yet I found a way to make it work.

"Who am I? Why, I am the wife who made a good marriage out of a bad one; I am Leah."

Genesis 29:16 *And Laban had two daughters: the name of the elder was Leah, and the name of the younger was Rachel.* **17** *Leah was tender eyed; but Rachel was beautiful and well favoured.* **18** *And Jacob loved Rachel; and said, I will serve thee seven years for Rachel thy younger daughter.* **19** *And Laban said, It is better that I give her to thee, than that I should give her to another man: abide with me.* **20** *And Jacob served seven years for Rachel; and they seemed unto him but a few days, for the love he had to her.* **21** *And Jacob said unto Laban, Give me my wife, for my days are fulfilled, that I may go in unto her.* **22** *And Laban gathered together all the men of the place, and made a feast.* **23** *And it came to pass in the evening, that he took Leah his daughter, and brought her to him; and he went in unto her.* **24** *And Laban gave unto his daughter Leah Zilpah his maid for an handmaid.* **25a** *And it came to pass, that in the morning, behold, it was Leah...*

The marriage before us may well be one of the most important ones in all of the Bible for us to study. You see, this marriage did not start off well, not at all! That makes it a prime case study for us, since a great many marriages in our modern world also do not start off well. If you are, by chance, in a marriage like that, there is hope! Leah took a marriage that started off unimaginably bad and somehow turned it into a very good marriage!

How did this remarkable woman turn a bad marriage into a good one?

She loved a flawed husband

Much can and has been and will be said about Leah and her flaws. But, friends, have you ever stopped to consider the flaws of the man that she chose to love?

Jacob was a mama's boy.

Genesis 25:28 *And Isaac loved Esau, because he did eat of his venison: but Rebekah loved Jacob.*

Jacob was a con artist.

Genesis 27:15 *And Rebekah took goodly raiment of her eldest son Esau, which were with her in the house, and put them upon Jacob her younger son:* **16** *And she put the skins of the kids of the goats upon his hands, and upon the smooth of his neck:* **17** *And she gave the savoury meat and the bread, which she had prepared, into the hand of her son Jacob.* **18** *And he came unto his father, and said, My father: and he said, Here am I; who art thou, my son?* **19** *And Jacob said unto his father, I am Esau thy firstborn; I have done according as thou badest me: arise, I pray thee, sit and eat of my venison, that thy soul may bless me.* **20** *And Isaac said unto his son, How is it that thou hast found it so quickly, my son? And he said, Because the LORD thy God brought it to me.* **21** *And Isaac said unto Jacob, Come near, I pray thee, that I may feel thee, my son, whether thou be my very son Esau or not.* **22** *And Jacob went near unto Isaac his father; and he felt him, and said, The voice is Jacob's voice, but the hands are the hands of Esau.* **23** *And he discerned him not, because his hands were hairy, as his brother Esau's hands: so he blessed him.* **24** *And he said, Art thou my very son Esau? And he said, I am.*

Jacob was also a "run and hide" man when trouble came. Both during his trouble with Esau and then later with Laban, he demonstrated this flaw.

In addition to all of that, he was, at this point, dirt poor, too! Look at what he said years later:

Genesis 32:10 *I am not worthy of the least of all the mercies, and of all the truth, which thou hast shewed unto thy servant; for with my staff I passed over this Jordan; and now I am become two bands.*

When Leah met Jacob and fell in love with him, do you know the entire summary of everything he owned in this world? A stick. He owned a stick.

Jacob was not exactly a catch for a woman! Yet she chose to love him, flaws and all.

Please notice that I said "flaws;" I did not say "lost." I say that because of what I know carnal people will be thinking to themselves if we do not head it off at the pass. "Well, Preacher, I know he is lost, but I choose to marry him despite that flaw."

That is not a flaw; it is a forbidden decision.

2 Corinthians 6:14 *Be ye not unequally yoked together with unbelievers: for what fellowship hath righteousness with unrighteousness? and what communion hath light with darkness?*

It is off limits! Jacob, for all of his flaws, was at least a believer.

Leah chose to love a man with flaws, lots of them.

Ma'am, if you cannot love a man with flaws, then you are going to be a marriage breaker rather than a marriage maker. This may surprise you, but there are no perfect men. And you better be glad of that, because if all men were perfect, then none of them would have anything to do with you!

Are you really so prideful as to think that you yourself have no flaws? One very obvious reason that Leah was willing to love Jacob despite his flaws is that she was painfully aware of her own.

I have absolutely lost count of the number of times a woman has sat with me and my wife during counseling, admitted that her husband is not cheating on her and is not abusing her, and yet tells me that she cannot live with him. It is clear that it is not that she cannot, it is that she WILL NOT. It is that she has chosen to disobey God and to break her vows.

Ladies, Leah loved a man that was far more flawed than whomever you are married to. Hello, polygamist/sissy/liar/mama's boy! But by the time they had been married a good while, he actually turned into a guy brave enough to wrestle with an angel! Her love helped to change him!

Ma'am, anyone can love a man with the physique of Arnold Schwarzenegger and the voice of Barry White and the romantic streak of Romeo, but that is not who you married. You married a real man, with real good points and real flaws.

And Ma'am, whoever the new guy is that wants to have you after you have been married for years, please remember something, your husband knows you and still wants you. Any new guy does not know you, and once he does the whole equation will change for him. Anyone trying to steal the affection of a married woman is someone who is just playing, and that is not the kind of man that will be around for you once you get old.

Leah was able to go from being young with her husband, to middle aged with her husband, to old with her husband for one very important reason–she chose to love a flawed husband.

Everything she ever did let her husband know how badly she wanted to be with him

How badly do you want to be with someone when you pretend to be your sister and marry them under those pretenses? Think of what that was like.

But it did not stop there. We will not elaborate on this just yet, but look at Genesis 30:16:

33

Genesis 30:16 *And Jacob came out of the field in the evening, and Leah went out to meet him, and said, Thou must come in unto me; for surely I have hired thee with my son's mandrakes. And he lay with her that night.*

This woman was very good at communicating to her husband that she wanted very badly to be with him!

Ladies, how many of you have ever made an "ego joke" about men? Do you know why people tell ego jokes about men? Because in general, men have egos. God made them like that just as surely as he made you to cry for no good reason.

Leah understood this about men. By constantly communicating to him how much she wanted to be with him, he ended up falling in love with her.

Ma'am, the grocery list is not the most important thing to communicate to your husband. The fact that he left his clothes on the floor and needs to pick them up is not the most important thing to communicate to your husband. The list of things that need fixing around the house is not the most important thing to communicate to your husband. The list of ways that he has upset you is not the most important thing to communicate to your husband. The complaints you have about his parenting skills are not the most important thing to communicate to your husband. Whatever it is that you feel inclined to harp on today is not the most important thing to communicate to your husband.

The most important thing you can ever communicate to your husband is the fact that you very badly want to be with him. And just like Leah, you will find that can and should be communicated both verbally and non-verbally.

On her "impromptu wedding night" she obviously did not communicate it verbally, or she would have been discovered!

During the episode with the mandrakes, she did communicate it verbally.

Ma'am, make sure that the look on your face always tells him that you want to be with him.

Ma'am, make sure that your tone of voice always tells him that you want to be with him.

Ma'am, make sure that you very often tell him verbally that you want to be with him.

Ma'am, make sure that the way you behave in the bedroom tells him that you want to be with him.

In that particularly, if that ever seems to him like it is a chore to you or a bother to you, then I can just about promise you that your marriage is headed for trouble and probably for divorce.

She loved a man who hated her

Not all women have to go through something so hard. When they do, it is sometimes, as it was in the case of Leah, the result of something that they have done. And no, I am not just guessing that Jacob hated Leah, the Bible actually tells us that he did.

Genesis 29:31 *And when the LORD saw that Leah was hated, he opened her womb: but Rachel was barren.*

I am not justifying this, but there is no denying that Leah brought this on herself. She tricked Jacob into marrying her, and he was trapped. Because of that, he hated her!

We see quite often ladies who have earned the hatred of their husbands. Often it is by cheating on them. Ladies, I cannot begin to adequately tell you just what this does to a man. The Bible puts it this way:

Proverbs 6:27 *Can a man take fire in his bosom, and his clothes not be burned? 28 Can one go upon hot coals, and his feet not be burned? 29 So he that goeth in to his neighbour's wife; whosoever toucheth her shall not be innocent. 30 Men do not despise a thief, if he steal to satisfy his soul when he is hungry; 31 But if he be found, he shall* *restore sevenfold; he shall give all the substance of his house.* **32** *But whoso committeth adultery with a woman lacketh understanding: he that doeth it destroyeth his own soul.* **33** *A wound and dishonour shall he get; and his reproach shall not be wiped away.* **34** *For jealousy is the rage of a man: therefore he will not spare in the day of vengeance.* **35** *He will not regard any ransom; neither will he rest content, though thou givest many gifts.*

Notice those words *jealousy, rage, vengeance.* Notice also that no amount of money or gifts can ever stop the man's desire to destroy someone or something when this has happened.

A man who has been cheated on has a very, very difficult time ever getting past it. Can it be done? Yes, of course. But are you going to have to be dealing with a husband who hates you for quite a while and the other guy forever? Probably.

Whatever the reason that a husband hates a wife, the example of Leah teaches us that it can be overcome. Leah is one of the greatest marriage makers ever, because she chose to love a man who hated her.

She kept things interesting

This is one of my favorite passages in the Bible:

Genesis 30:14 *And Reuben went in the days of wheat harvest, and found mandrakes in the field, and brought them unto his mother Leah. Then Rachel said to Leah, Give me, I pray thee, of thy son's mandrakes.* **15** *And she said unto her, Is it a small matter that thou hast taken my husband? and wouldest thou take away my son's mandrakes also? And Rachel said, Therefore he shall lie with thee to night for thy son's mandrakes.* **16** *And Jacob came out of the field in the evening, and Leah went out to meet him, and said, Thou must come in unto me; for surely I have hired thee with my son's mandrakes. And he lay with her that night.*

When little Reuben came home from the field that day, he was carrying a gift for mommy. He had found a bunch of mandrakes. Another name for them is "love apples." They were yellow in color, and they had a strong and beautiful smell. They were among the most prized of fruits. They were used as an aphrodisiac, and women would fight for them like cats and dogs.

Rachel saw them, and she wanted some. Jacob was at work out in the field somewhere; he did not have a clue that there was anything odd going on at home. Rachel and Leah went round and round over them, and they ended up striking a bargain. Leah gave Rachel the mandrakes, and Rachel agreed to let Leah have Jacob for the night.

This is hysterical to me. Jacob did not have a clue what was going on, but back home his wives were having an auction for "his services" that night!

Jacob came home, and here is what happened:

Genesis 30:16 *And Jacob came out of the field in the evening, and Leah went out to meet him, and said, Thou must come in unto me; for surely I have hired thee with my son's mandrakes. And he lay with her that night.*

Ladies, would you not agree that this is the most unorthodox, out of the blue, unexpected thing imaginable? In other words, it was interesting!

How many of you have ever heard my ten commandments of marital intimacy? Let me give them to you:

Thou shalt not be boring.
Thou shalt not be boring.
Thou shalt not be boring.
Thou shalt not be boring.
Thou shalt not be boring.
Thou shalt not be boring.
Thou shalt not be boring.
Thou shalt not be boring.

37

Thou shalt not be boring.

Thou really, really shalt not be boring.

I am not making these up. I am simply paraphrasing a Biblical principle:

Genesis 26:8 *And it came to pass, when he had been there a long time, that Abimelech king of the Philistines looked out at a window, and saw, and, behold, Isaac was* ***sporting*** *with Rebekah his wife.*

Golf was invented in about A.D. 1200. Basketball is just over a hundred years old. Baseball is about two hundred years old. Isaac and Rebekah were married about 3,500 years ago. They were not playing golf, or basketball, or football, or soccer, or cricket, or tennis, or any other modern sport. But they were playing. That word sporting is the Hebrew word *tsawchak*. It indicates to play sexually, and one of its primary definitions is to make a toy of another. These two got very creative. Maybe a little too creative being as how someone else managed to see them! You say, "Preacher, that is awful!" Yes, I agree. But it is obvious they did not mean to be seen, so I am willing to cut them some slack. But do you know what is really awful? People that are so very careful and reserved and boring and dull that their marriage dies a slow, silent death. Friends, for all of Isaac and Rebekah's faults, they at least got this right, their undefiled bed was a bed of creativity and intrigue and excitement. When the king catches you at it, you are living life on the edge!

Ladies, keep things interesting. Rachel was by far the prettier of the two, but Leah was easily the more interesting of the two. Jacob very quickly knew exactly what to expect from Rachel: a pouty, self-absorbed, spoiled brat. But with Leah he never knew what to expect from her from day to day. But whatever it was, it always turned out to be something good, and it always turned out to be something that benefitted him.

Ladies, what is the last unexpected, exciting thing you ever did to make your husband go, "Whoaaaa!" and how often do you do something like that? Marriage makers make a habit of it.

She may not have been pretty, but she knew how to be alluring

Let me show you something amazing, something that follows up on the episode with the mandrakes:

Genesis 30:17 *And God hearkened unto Leah, and she conceived, and bare Jacob the fifth son.* **18** *And Leah said, God hath given me my hire, because I have given my maiden to my husband: and she called his name Issachar.* **19** *And Leah conceived again, and bare Jacob the sixth son.* **20** *And Leah said, God hath endued me with a good dowry; now will my husband dwell with me, because I have born him six sons: and she called his name Zebulun.* **21** *And afterwards she bare a daughter, and called her name Dinah.*

Leah gave all the mandrakes to Rachel to draw Jacob to herself. She got pregnant and had a son named Issachar. End of story, right? After all, no more mandrakes! But lo and behold, the next thing we read is that more than nine months later, Leah conceived again, had a boy, and named him Zebulun. Then lo and behold, after those nine months are up, she conceives again and has a daughter named Dinah. In other words, when there were no more mandrakes, Jacob was still doing exactly what Leah wanted, he was hanging around and loving her.

Was Rachel not prettier? Yes, she was. But something about Leah kept drawing Jacob back to her. We call that "allurement." Ladies, you do not have to be a knockout to be alluring to your husband. In fact, when you think of the body, it may surprise you some of the parts the Bible describes as having the power of allurement.

Proverbs 6:24 *To keep thee from the evil woman, from the flattery of the tongue of a strange woman.* **25** *Lust not after her beauty in thine heart;* **neither let her take thee with her eyelids.**

There is awesome power of allurement just in the way that you can look at your husband. Ladies, you ought to try something from time to time. See if you can master the art of telling your husband that you desire his intimacy just by the kind of eye contact that you make with him.

Look at another thing the Bible describes as being alluring:

Proverbs 7:21 *With her much fair speech she caused him to yield, with the flattering of her lips she forced him.*

What you say and the tone of voice you say it in can have incredible alluring power to your husband.

I am not trying to be unkind, but I remember way back in my teenage years a rather unattractive girl who always seemed to have a guy. I did not understand it then, but now as an older and wiser person I do. For all of her really chronic bad looks, she knew what to say to make guys want her. She was wicked, and because of that I would never have anything to do with her, but she was successful at getting different guys to fall for her. Her words were alluring.

Ladies, use that power in your home with your husband. Leah was a marriage maker not because she was pretty; she was actually an unattractive woman. She was a marriage maker because she was alluring.

She stood out as a contrast against her unspiritual sister

When the story began, the only difference that Jacob seemed to see is that Leah was ugly and Rachel was pretty. But let me show you another episode that shows an even greater difference between them.

40

This episode happened years after Jacob and his wives had been married and after having had a bunch of kids. Jacob has decided to sneak off and run back to his home country. After a few days, Laban found out about it, and he gave chase and caught them. Pick up the story in Genesis 31:26.

Genesis 31:26 *And Laban said to Jacob, What hast thou done, that thou hast stolen away unawares to me, and carried away my daughters, as captives taken with the sword?* **27** *Wherefore didst thou flee away secretly, and steal away from me; and didst not tell me, that I might have sent thee away with mirth, and with songs, with tabret, and with harp?* **28** *And hast not suffered me to kiss my sons and my daughters? thou hast now done foolishly in so doing.* **29** *It is in the power of my hand to do you hurt: but the God of your father spake unto me yesternight, saying, Take thou heed that thou speak not to Jacob either good or bad.* **30** ***And now, though thou wouldest needs be gone, because thou sore longedst after thy father's house, yet wherefore hast thou stolen my gods?***

One reason Leah and Rachel's daddy, Laban, was so upset is because he was an idolater, and his gods were missing. Somebody had stolen his idols, and he figured it was Jacob. Pick it back up in the next verse:

31 *And Jacob answered and said to Laban, Because I was afraid: for I said, Peradventure thou wouldest take by force thy daughters from me.* **32** *With whomsoever thou findest thy gods, let him not live: before our brethren discern thou what is thine with me, and take it to thee.* ***For Jacob knew not that Rachel had stolen them.*** **33** *And Laban went into Jacob's tent, and into Leah's tent, and into the two maidservants' tents; but he found them not. Then went he out of Leah's tent, and entered into Rachel's tent.* **34** *Now Rachel had taken the images, and put them in the camel's furniture, and sat upon them. And Laban searched all the tent, but*

41

found them not. **35** *And she said to her father, Let it not displease my lord that I cannot rise up before thee; for the custom of women is upon me. And he searched, but found not the images.*

This is an excellent view of just how different Rachel and Leah were in the spiritual realm. Jacob was a believer in just one God, Jehovah. His wives knew that. But Rachel was so attached to the idols, the false gods of her daddy, that she stole them and took them with her. Then, as further proof of her spiritual bankruptcy, she lied about it, and even blamed her period on her failure to stand up before her father, when in fact she was sitting on the idols.

Rachel and Leah could not have been more different, especially in the spiritual realm.

Ladies, if you really want to be a marriage maker, be a spiritual woman. Do not make your husband have to fight to get you to be in church. Do not make your husband have to go to church alone. Do not be up and ready to go to a baby shower or a wedding or a birthday party or Walmart and then every Sunday decide that you are too sick to go to church.

The most miserable men I know are husbands that are trying to live for the Lord while their wives refuse to do the same. Ma'am, that is the behavior of a marriage breaker, not the behavior of a marriage maker.

Leah, oh Leah, what a woman. She was one of the best marriage makers ever, because she took a bad marriage and made a good marriage out of it! And how did it turn out for her? Fast forward a bunch of years. Jacob is about to die, and he has some instructions for his kids:

Genesis 49:29 *And he charged them, and said unto them, I am to be gathered unto my people: bury me with my fathers in the cave that is in the field of Ephron the Hittite,* **30** *In the cave that is in the field of Machpelah, which is before Mamre, in the land of Canaan, which Abraham*

42

*bought with the field of Ephron the Hittite for a possession of a buryingplace. **31** There they buried Abraham and Sarah his wife; there they buried Isaac and Rebekah his wife; and there I buried Leah.*

Jacob could have chosen to be buried beside either one. He chose Leah. He chose Leah…

Chapter 4
The Couple that Did Not Live
Happily Ever After

"And they lived happily ever after! How often had we two heard those words of others? And with the way our marriage began, we were both quite certain that ours would find such success as well. Some homes have the stress of trying to make ends meet. Our home never had that problem, since both of us were quite wealthy. Some homes have the stress of having to deal with a bad boss in the workplace. But when the head of the home is also the king of the nation, how can that ever be an issue?

"Our marriage was a true love affair from the word go. How many husbands have a wife that saves his life from her own father? How many wives have a husband that killed two hundred men just to earn her hand in marriage?

"Life in the palace was grand, marriage was good, and we truly were on our way to a happily ever after ending. But along the way, something most unfortunate happened...

"Our marriage was not undone by the usual suspects of infidelity or the growing boredom of long familiarity. No, our marriage was undone in an instant, in a moment of time and a flash of anger from both of us. If you can learn from us, please do, so that perhaps our foolishness will not be entirely in vain.

"Who are we? Why, we are the couple that did not live happily ever after; we are David and Michal."

2 Samuel 6:1 *Again, David gathered together all the chosen men of Israel, thirty thousand. 2 And David arose, and went with all the people that were with him from Baale of Judah, to bring up from thence the ark of God, whose name is called by the name of the LORD of hosts that dwelleth between the cherubims. 3 And they set the ark of God upon a new cart, and brought it out of the house of Abinadab that was in Gibeah: and Uzzah and Ahio, the sons of Abinadab, drave the new cart. 4 And they brought it out of the house of Abinadab which was at Gibeah, accompanying the ark of God: and Ahio went before the ark. 5 And David and all the house of Israel played before the LORD on all manner of instruments made of fir wood, even on harps, and on psalteries, and on timbrels, and on cornets, and on cymbals. 6 And when they came to Nachon's threshingfloor, Uzzah put forth his hand to the ark of God, and took hold of it; for the oxen shook it. 7 And the anger of the LORD was kindled against Uzzah; and God smote him there for his error; and there he died by the ark of God. 8 And David was displeased, because the LORD had made a breach upon Uzzah: and he called the name of the place Perezuzzah to this day. 9 And David was afraid of the LORD that day, and said, How shall the ark of the LORD come to me? 10 So David would not remove the ark of the LORD unto him into the city of David: but David carried it aside into the house of Obededom the Gittite. 11 And the ark of the LORD continued in the house of Obededom the Gittite three months: and the LORD blessed Obededom, and all his household. 12 And it was told king David, saying, The LORD hath blessed the house of Obededom, and all that pertaineth* *unto him, because of the ark of God. So David went and brought up the ark of God from the house of Obededom into the city of David with gladness.* **13** *And it was so, that when they that bare the ark of the LORD had gone six paces, he sacrificed oxen and fatlings.* **14** *And David danced before the LORD with all his might; and David was girded with a linen ephod.* **15** *So David and all the house of Israel brought up the ark of the LORD with shouting, and with the sound of the trumpet.* **16** *And as the ark of the LORD came into the city of David, Michal Saul's daughter looked through a window, and saw king David leaping and dancing before the LORD; and she despised him in her heart.* **17** *And they brought in the ark of the LORD, and set it in his place, in the midst of the tabernacle that David had pitched for it: and David offered burnt offerings and peace offerings before the LORD.* **18** *And as soon as David had made an end of offering burnt offerings and peace offerings, he blessed the people in the name of the LORD of hosts.* **19** *And he dealt among all the people, even among the whole multitude of Israel, as well to the women as men, to every one a cake of bread, and a good piece of flesh, and a flagon of wine. So all the people departed every one to his house.* **20** *Then David returned to bless his household. And Michal the daughter of Saul came out to meet David, and said, How glorious was the king of Israel to day, who uncovered himself to day in the eyes of the handmaids of his servants, as one of the vain fellows shamelessly uncovereth himself!* **21** *And David said unto Michal, It was before the LORD, which chose me before thy father, and before all his house, to appoint me ruler over the people of the LORD, over Israel: therefore will I play before the LORD.* **22** *And I will yet be more vile than thus, and will be base in mine own sight: and of the maidservants which thou hast spoken of, of them shall I be had in honour.* **23** *Therefore Michal the daughter of Saul had no child unto the day of her death.*

As was read in the letter above, this couple of marriage breakers was an absolute tragedy. They really did love each other, and they started their marriage off with an amazing passion. Yet their marriage fell in about sixty seconds of time! This was one of the most dramatic destructions of a home the world has ever witnessed.

You will notice that I included the entire chapter, even though the marriage was destroyed in verses sixteen through twenty-three. The reason I did that was to include the text that gives the context of what happened.

When Israel was freed from Egypt hundreds of years earlier by God through Moses, God took them out into the wilderness and taught them how He expected to be worshipped. One of the vital parts of that worship was a special piece of furniture called the Ark of the Covenant, or the Ark of God. It was a wooden box covered in gold, with a couple of golden angels mounted on top of it. While it was in the wilderness tabernacle, the very presence of God would rest on it. It was literally the spot where God would meet with His people.

But the children of Israel disobeyed God, and because of that, during the days of Eli the Priest, before there ever was a king in Israel, they lost the Ark in a battle with the Philistines. The Philistines, for their part, did not know what to do or not do with it, and God ended up killing a great many of them. So they loaded it up onto a cart and shipped it back to the Israelites!

It is then that something unimaginable happened. The children of Israel basically forgot that it even existed.

In 1 Samuel 7 we find that it ended up in the house of a man named Abinadab. This thing which should have been the centerpiece of the entire nation became a dust collector in the house of one man.

Verse two tells us that it was there for twenty years before anyone even began to mourn for it and for God. After that period of twenty years we come to 1 Samuel 8-9, where the people demanded and received a king. That king's name was Saul, and according to Acts 13:21 he ruled for forty years. All that time, the ark was still in the house of Abinidab. Finally, after Saul, David became king. Somewhere in the early years of the reign of David, we come to 2 Samuel 6, and we find David finally bringing the Ark back out into the nation again and setting up a house for it. In other words, it had been gone for, at the very least, sixty years! Sixty years! The most important object in Jewish life had been gone since before David was born!

But in our text, David went and got it. This was the greatest day of celebration the Jews had ever known since the days of the Exodus. David was ecstatic, the people were ecstatic, David was leaping and dancing, everyone was praising God.

Well, almost everyone.

David's wife, Michal, was not among the "happy people" at that moment. In fact, she was very unhappy. And when David came home, happy, she unloaded all of her unhappy!

In the blink of an eye David was unhappy right along with her. And within sixty seconds time, their marriage was destroyed. That was bad news for them, but in a way, it is good news for us. It gives us the chance to look at the entire situation and figure out what they did wrong. And if we can do that, we will know what things we ought not to be doing in our own marriages!

So let's jump in.

The first mistake they made was one of separation
2 Samuel 6:15 *So David and all the house of Israel brought up the ark of the LORD with shouting, and with the sound of the trumpet.*

49

There is a very important phrase to take note of in this verse, the phrase "and all the house of Israel." This was the biggest, most important thing that had happened for literally hundreds of years, and everyone turned out for it. This was King David's greatest moment, greater even than his victory over Goliath, and as such, all of his people were there to celebrate this great accomplishment along with their king.

But maybe you are thinking that this was just a "man thing," and that all the women-folk were left at home doing "women stuff." If you think that, you would be wrong:

2 Samuel 6:19 *And he dealt among all the people, even among the whole multitude of Israel, as well to the women as men, to every one a cake of bread, and a good piece of flesh, and a flagon of wine. So all the people departed every one to his house.*

God very specifically included that phrase in this verse *as well to the women as men* to let us know that even all of the women had turned out for this great event!

Well maybe it was just certain important women! No again, because verse twenty mentions maidservants. The picture that God has very carefully drawn for us is one in which every man, woman, and child in the nation had turned out for this once in a millennium kind of event!

Out of the entire nation, do you realize that there is only one person that we know for a certainty was not there?

2 Samuel 6:16a *And as the ark of the LORD came into the city of David, Michal Saul's daughter looked through a window...*

Maybe possibly there was someone else who was not there, but it does not sound like it. The only person in the nation that we know for a fact was still indoors was Michal, the wife of the guy out there who was so happy that he was dancing in the street!

Somehow, for some reason, a separation had begun to grow in the relationship of Michal and David.

There are two possible culprits. One, it could be that David had her to stay home for some reason. The only other option is that she herself chose to stay home. Either way, the result was the same: something that mattered to David was something that she was not involved in. Two people that used to be so very close had somehow allowed a separation to begin growing between them.

Things that are important or enjoyable to women are not usually that important or enjoyable to men, and things that are important or enjoyable to men are not usually important or enjoyable to women.

That is very dangerous.

Whatever is important to the one you love ought to be important to you as well, as long as it is not sinful. You may not understand it; most men do not understand "browsing malls," nor do most women understand "chasing a little white ball around with a stick." But the time together is more important than "understanding what it is about this he/she could possibly like."

Two very good pastor friends of mine are both blessed in their marriage. They both have wives that have chosen to participate in what their husband does and loves, which is hunting. Both of those ladies will get up early in the morning with their man, hike out into the cold woods, crawl up in a deer stand, and sit there quietly for hours. Neither of those ladies really care for hunting. But they care for their husbands who do care for hunting.

I get a kick out of listening to a dear older gentleman in my church tell me about going to shop with his wife at a store called Hamrick's. He usually ends up in the "men's waiting area," but he is there at Hamrick's with his wife.

Many times, I have been to Mary Jo's Fabric Store with my wife Dana. I hate fabric stores. But I love my wife!

51

Even in the things that you do not or cannot participate in, husbands and wives, you should still at least discuss it and learn about it.

My wife does Pilates. Mark this down, I am not doing Pilates. Ever. If I am anywhere that there are steel weights laying around, I am not going to be caught dead doing "The Rolling Ball."

But I know what the Rolling Ball is! I ask her about Pilates, and have learned enough that I can somewhat intelligently discuss it with her.

There are so many things that drive wedges of separation in between husbands and wives. And listen to me very carefully, the whole thing about a wedge is, it starts very small at the point. But the farther you drive it in, the wider the separation gets. If there is something that is causing a separation, then either both need to get involved with it or the one involved needs to give it up.

I know of a marriage right now between actual adults, and I mean people older than me, where the husband comes home from work every day, heads straight for the bedroom, turns on his video games, and plays them until the wee hours of the morning. Video games have caused a separation in their marriage, and even though they are still living under the same roof, their marriage is basically non-existent.

So let me say it again, if there is something that is causing a separation, if there is something that is driving a wedge, then either both need to get involved with it or the one involved needs to give it up. Do you remember the very first descriptive phrase that God used of man and wife?

Genesis 2:24 *Therefore shall a man leave his father and his mother, and shall cleave unto his wife: and they shall be **one flesh**.*

David and Michal's first mistake was one of separation.

52

The second mistake they made was one of irritation

2 Samuel 6:16 *And as the ark of the LORD came into the city of David, Michal Saul's daughter looked through a window, and saw king David leaping and dancing before the LORD;* ***and she despised him in her heart.***

The phrase "in her heart" is an important one. It lets us know that she had not yet begun to spout off about any ill feelings that she had toward him. In other words, she was what we would call "irritated" at David. She was not yet screaming or throwing things; she had just developed a very bad inner attitude toward him.

Now you are probably thinking, "But wait a minute, Preacher, you cannot control whether or not you get irritated at someone! It just happens!"

Maybe. But even if that is true, you most certainly can control how you handle that irritation. In the vast majority of cases, husbands and wives handle their irritation pretty much just like Michal did; they wait for the first available opportunity and then they blow a gasket. How many of you will admit that you have done that from time to time? And how well did that work out for you? Not good, I would guess.

Here is the thing about Michal's irritation and most likely about all of your irritation with your spouse, too, when everything is "weighed in the balance," there really was not and is not much of a reason to be irritated! For whatever reason, Michal got really ill with David for his dance before the Lord. But may I tell you what she clearly was not thinking about at that moment?

David was a good provider...

David was brave...

David loved her...

David loved the Lord!

If she had weighed all of that out, she would have lost that irritation pretty quickly. Her attitude toward him would have softened immediately.

Ladies, do you sometimes get irritated with your husband? You know, the clothes laying around, the pig headedness, the "maleness?"

Men, do you sometimes get irritated with your wife? You know, the roller coaster ride of emotions, the illogical thought process, the "femaleness?"

But if someone came into your home and pointed a gun at your spouse, you would immediately jump in between them, because you instinctively know that there is a lot more good than bad, and that you are about to lose something very valuable and precious!

Do you know what a lot of couples ought to do? You ought to go buy a little old fashioned scale, with the little tray on each side and the rod in the middle, and just put it somewhere visible in your home, as a reminder for the next time you get irritated with your husband or wife. Cool the irritation down, let it go, because what you have in your spouse is a lot bigger and better and more important than any little irritation that you have with them.

The third mistake they made was one of accusation

2 Samuel 6:20 *Then David returned to bless his household. And Michal the daughter of Saul came out to meet David, and said,* ***How glorious was the king of Israel to day, who uncovered himself to day in the eyes of the handmaids of his servants, as one of the vain fellows shamelessly uncovereth himself!***

Men, try your best to put yourself in David's shoes right at that exact moment. Michal has just, out of the blue, made a huge accusation against him! He was completely blindsided. And look at the adjectives she used to accompany this accusation: *glorious... vain... shameless...*

54

And the accusation itself? That he "uncovered" himself before all those women in the street. That word means exactly what you think; it indicates nakedness!

Please follow this with me. Is there or is there not a HUGE crowd of people in the street? Yes. In the midst of that crowd, David is leaping and dancing before the Lord. When he gets home, she accuses him of being naked. But do you remember something that God Himself noted in an earlier verse?

2 Samuel 6:14 *And David danced before the LORD with all his might; **and David was girded with a linen ephod.***

In other words, David did have clothes on. What very obvious thing has happened? Michal has looked out of the window into that huge crowd, she has seen enough to realize that David is leaping and dancing, but she has then *assumed* that he is not dressed! Her view was obviously not as good as she thought it was. So when David came home, she blew up at him and threw an accusation up in his face.

Was there a better way? Yes, there was. David's son Solomon wrote about it many years later.

Proverbs 18:13 *He that answereth a matter before he heareth it, it is folly and shame unto him.*

Michal could have chosen to ask questions and hear the answers before she jumped to conclusions and made an accusation. But once the accusation was made, it could not be "unmade." To quote it in legal terms, "you cannot unring a bell."

A thousand years or so later Paul in 1 Corinthians 13:5 said that love *thinketh no evil.* Love chooses not to jump to conclusions, love chooses not to make accusations, love chooses to ask questions and then carefully listen to the answer.

55

The fourth mistake was one of escalation

2 Samuel 6:21 *And David said unto Michal, It was before the LORD,* **which chose me before thy father, and before all his house**, *to appoint me ruler over the people of the LORD, over Israel: therefore will I play before the LORD.*

David did not even bother to answer her false accusation. What she said and what she accused him of got him so immediately furious that all he was interested in was blowing up right back at her. And when he did, he did not blow up in an "eye for an eye" manner; that would have been bad enough. No, he blew up in an "eye, tooth, arm, leg, kidney, and spleen for an eye" manner. David chose to escalate this fight into a nuclear battle. Look again at what he said:

2 Samuel 6:21 *It was before the LORD,* **which chose me before thy father, and before all his house**, *to appoint me ruler over the people of the LORD, over Israel: therefore will I play before the LORD.*

Before this exact moment, how many people had been involved in their argument? Just two, him and her. But now David reaches way back into the past and brings her entire family into it. He basically said, "I am better than your stinkin' failure of a daddy, I am better than your worthless brothers and cousins and aunts and uncles and sisters and grandpas! God chose me and threw all of those losers in your family to the curb!"

Well that is sure to fix things right up, now isn't it!

Uhhhh, no. All that is going to do is make matters much, much, much, much, much, much worse!

Husbands, wives, take heed. In wartime, if you are attacked, it is absolutely necessary to escalate things. Why? Because your goal is to win, and to do that you need to break and/or destroy your enemy. But you are not in a war. You are in a marriage. That person you wake up beside each day is not your enemy, that is the other half of you. There is not one reason, ever, to escalate a fight in your marriage. Escalation is always designed to break or destroy.

In every fight or argument in marriage, every word out of your mouth ought to be aimed toward "de-escalation." In every fight or argument in marriage, every word out of your mouth ought to be aimed toward getting things settled down rather than stirred up even farther.

Lower your voice.

Speak in kind terms.

Never insult.

Never bring others into it the way that David did.

So very often homes break up, and when you question why, they say, "Oh it was over some little thing!" But if you check carefully, it probably did not actually break up over the little thing. It probably broke up over the escalation that followed the little thing.

The fifth mistake was one of retaliation .

2 Samuel 6:22 *And I will yet be more vile than thus, and will be base in mine own sight: and of the maidservants which thou hast spoken of, of them shall I be had in honour.* **23** *Therefore Michal the daughter of Saul had no child unto the day of her death.*

Michal and David allowed a separation to grow between them. Then Michal got irritated with David. Then she made an accusation against him. But is there anything in the text that says she wanted the marriage to end? Is there anything in the text that says she never wanted David to touch her again? No. That is not what she wanted. She loved David, and she was the wife of a king. All she wanted to do was blow up at him. I am guessing that ten seconds after she did it, she was already beginning to feel better because she had "gotten it off her chest."

She was done at that moment. But David was not done. First he escalated, then he retaliated. The way he retaliated was to put her away and never touch her again. She was still legally married to him but was as good as divorced, because he never did behave as a husband to her again. She was like some servant girl in the palace, just another person to cook and clean. David retaliated, and his retaliation was the nail in the coffin of their marriage.

You cannot imagine how many times a pastor or marriage counselor sees this.

One cheats, so the other does.

One hits, so the other does.

One cusses, so the other does.

One talks bad about the spouse at work, so the other does.

I have ten fingers and I can count on none of them, how many marriages have ever been fixed by retaliation. In the history of mankind, no marriages have ever been "fixed" by means of retaliation. Do you realize that all David had to do to make sure that eventually things would get back to normal is just not retaliate? He could have taken a walk to cool down. He could have not spoken to her for a few days. He could have gone off to battle for a while. He had plenty of options other than retaliation! But once he retaliated, he did so in such a way as to end it all.

Five chances. They had five chances to head this off at the pass. She could have been with him out there in the street, but she was not. She could have weighed out everything she knew about him and let go of her irritation, but she did not. She could have asked questions, but instead, she made accusations. He could have de-escalated the argument, but he escalated it instead. He could have chosen to walk away and cool off, but he chose to retaliate.

They had five chances to live happily ever after, and they blew every...single...one of them.

Chapter 5
The Man Who Wrote the Song
"Breaking Up Isn't Hard to Do"

"Greetings mere commoners, assembled on such a day. It is your privilege to hear from me, of that I have no doubt. Please try to contain your thrill as my words come ringing into your unworthy ears.

"I was a man who had it all. Wealth, power, prestige, and my choice of women to wed, and wed I did. As king, it was expected that I would have a queen, and no ordinary woman would do for such an extraordinary man as myself. And so it was that I married a dashing woman, well favored, desired by all.

"Naturally, she could not comprehend how very lucky she was to have a man such as myself. What woman could? The mind of a woman is such a small thing, after all, and that is why they are to be dominated, ordered about, kept in their place.

"And that is exactly what I did with my wife, my property.

"Until THAT day! Who would ever have dreamed such a thing could happen? Apparently I had been far too good to her, because when I made one simple request of her, she refused it! I was enraged, enraged, I tell you! How dare she not parade before my drunken friends and arouse their lust when I demanded it!

"Out of place! The woman was out of place! And I was just the man to put her back in that place! And I did. I made her pay for her insolence. I divorced her and banished her from being queen. That, you common simpletons, THAT is how you handle a woman!

"Who am I? Why, I am that man who wrote the song 'Breaking Up Isn't Hard to Do;' I am Ahasuerus."

Esther 1:1 *Now it came to pass in the days of Ahasuerus, (this is Ahasuerus which reigned, from India even unto Ethiopia, over an hundred and seven and twenty provinces:)* **2** *That in those days, when the king Ahasuerus sat on the throne of his kingdom, which was in Shushan the palace,* **3** *In the third year of his reign, he made a feast unto all his princes and his servants; the power of Persia and Media, the nobles and princes of the provinces, being before him:* **4** *When he shewed the riches of his glorious kingdom and the honour of his excellent majesty many days, even an hundred and fourscore days.* **5** *And when these days were expired, the king made a feast unto all the people that were present in Shushan the palace, both unto great and small, seven days, in the court of the garden of the king's palace;* **6** *Where were white, green, and blue, hangings, fastened with cords of fine linen and purple to silver rings and pillars of marble: the beds were of gold and silver, upon a pavement of red, and blue, and white, and black, marble.* **7** *And they gave them drink in vessels of gold, (the vessels being diverse one from another,) and royal wine in abundance, according to the state of the king.* **8** *And the drinking was according to the law; none did compel: for so the king had appointed to all the officers of his house, that they should do according to every man's pleasure.* **9** *Also Vashti the queen made a feast for the women in the royal house which belonged to king*

Ahasuerus. **10** *On the seventh day, when the heart of the king was merry with wine, he commanded Mehuman, Biztha, Harbona, Bigtha, and Abagtha, Zethar, and Carcas, the seven chamberlains that served in the presence of Ahasuerus the king,* **11** *To bring Vashti the queen before the king with the crown royal, to shew the people and the princes her beauty: for she was fair to look on.* **12** *But the queen Vashti refused to come at the king's commandment by his chamberlains: therefore was the king very wroth, and his anger burned in him.* **13** *Then the king said to the wise men, which knew the times, (for so was the king's manner toward all that knew law and judgment:* **14** *And the next unto him was Carshena, Shethar, Admatha, Tarshish, Meres, Marsena, and Memucan, the seven princes of Persia and Media, which saw the king's face, and which sat the first in the kingdom;)* **15** *What shall we do unto the queen Vashti according to law, because she hath not performed the commandment of the king Ahasuerus by the chamberlains?* **16** *And Memucan answered before the king and the princes, Vashti the queen hath not done wrong to the king only, but also to all the princes, and to all the people that are in all the provinces of the king Ahasuerus.* **17** *For this deed of the queen shall come abroad unto all women, so that they shall despise their husbands in their eyes, when it shall be reported, The king Ahasuerus commanded Vashti the queen to be brought in before him, but she came not.* **18** *Likewise shall the ladies of Persia and Media say this day unto all the king's princes, which have heard of the deed of the queen. Thus shall there arise too much contempt and wrath.* **19** *If it please the king, let there go a royal commandment from him, and let it be written among the laws of the Persians and the Medes, that it be not altered, That Vashti come no more before king Ahasuerus; and let the king give her royal estate unto another that is better than she.* **20** *And when the king's decree which he shall make shall be published throughout* *all his empire, (for it is great,) all the wives shall give to their husbands honour, both to great and small.* **21** *And the saying pleased the king and the princes; and the king did according to the word of Memucan:* **22** *For he sent letters into all the king's provinces, into every province according to the writing thereof, and to every people after their language, that every man should bear rule in his own house, and that it should be published according to the language of every people.*

We have before us the case of one King Ahasuerus, and his wife/former wife, Vashti. He was the king of the Persian Empire, which at that time was the most powerful nation on earth. That made him the most powerful man on earth. Most of the book of Esther is dedicated to the wife of his second marriage, Esther, and to how she saved the Jewish people from an evil plot.

But before there was a Queen Esther, there was Queen Vashti. And as great as Esther was, Vashti was pretty great in her own right. This was a remarkable woman, a woman that a man would be lucky to be married to. She was beautiful, proper, strong, and smart. But despite all of that, this was a marriage that ended up broken. And I want to make one thing very, very clear right up front: it was his fault.

I have been amazed through the years at the people that have made Vashti out to be the one at fault in this sordid affair. What has really amazed me is that most of the time, the people defending Ahasuerus and ripping into Vashti are women! In every case it has been some woman who has been brainwashed into thinking that a husband is always right even when he is wrong, and that it is somehow right to obey your husband even if it means disobeying God in the process.

If you are one of those folks, then I promise you, you are very quickly going to become very unhappy with this chapter. Ahasuerus was a first rate jerk. And it was not Vashti that divorced him; it was Ahasuerus that divorced her.

When a man is right and a woman is wrong, I am going to say so. But when a woman is right and man is wrong, I am going to say so then, too. This guy had a huge multi-faceted attitude problem. His attitude destroyed a home. His attitude made him a marriage breaker rather than a marriage maker.

So let's work our way through this text and find out what kind of attitude problem Ahasuerus had that made him a marriage breaker.

He had an attitude of entitlement

Esther 1:1 *Now it came to pass in the days of Ahasuerus, (this is Ahasuerus which reigned, from India even unto Ethiopia, over an hundred and seven and twenty provinces:)*

The book of Esther begins by introducing us to a king, a man by the name of Ahasuerus. The name he is more commonly known by to historians is Xerxes. Please allow me to tell you just a bit about him, because once you know what kind of a man he was, the things you read about in the book of Esther will make much more sense.

Xerxes was a man who had both a soft side and a brutally hard side. On the soft side he loved luxury; he loved living the good life. He was a womanizer, even though the law of the Medes and Persians forbid it. In other words, he felt like his position entitled him to whatever he wanted, whenever he wanted it, even if it was something wrong. That is why you see him doing this just a few verses later:

Esther 1:10 *On the seventh day, when the heart of the king was merry with wine, he commanded Mehuman, Biztha, Harbona, Bigtha, and Abagtha, Zethar, and Carcas, the seven chamberlains that served in the presence of*

Ahasuerus the king, **11** *To bring Vashti the queen before the king with the crown royal, to shew the people and the princes her beauty: for she was fair to look on.*

What Ahasuerus demanded in this passage was expressly forbidden by all of the laws and expectations of the Persian culture. His demand was that Vashti come and parade her beauty before all of those leering, drunken men. I have said, and I stand by my statement, that it was wrong in every way. Now please allow me to tell you how it was wrong in every way.

It was wrong morally. This one should be obvious to everyone.

Matthew 5:28 *But I say unto you, That whosoever looketh on a woman to lust after her hath committed adultery with her already in his heart.*

It was wrong maritally, to demand that a wife arouse the lust of men to whom she was not married and to have that demand made by her own husband! According to Ephesians 5, a husband is to work to present his wife to himself, not to others!

It was also wrong culturally. The custom of the Persians did not allow for a woman to appear in public.

It was wrong due to their royal station as well. According to Persian customs the queen, even more than the wives of other men, was secluded from the public gaze.

In every way imaginable, what Ahasuerus asked was dead wrong. Vashti knew it, and she responded accordingly. Ahasuerus knew it too, but he did not care. Why? He had an attitude of entitlement. Whatever he wanted he ought to be given it, whenever he wanted it, regardless of how it impacted others.

Men, that kind of a poison attitude will kill your marriage. That kind of attitude is the exact opposite of the attitude which God commanded us to have.

Philippians 2:3 *Let nothing be done through strife or vainglory; but in lowliness of mind let each esteem other better than themselves.* **4** *Look not every man on his own things, but every man also on the things of others.*

This applies to the husband and wife relationship as well as to every other relationship. The text does not say, "Let nothing be done through strife or vainglory, unless it is how the husband treats his wife; but in lowliness of mind let each esteem other better than themselves, except for how the husband treats his wife. Look not every man on his own things, but every man also on the things of others, unless it is his wife."

No, these two verses include how the husband treats his wife. The husband is to esteem his wife as better than himself. The husband is to look first to how things will affect his wife, before he ever considers how it will affect him. That kind of an attitude, sir, will make a marriage, but the entitlement attitude that Ahasuerus had will break a marriage.

Sir, your wife is not your property; she is your mate. She is not your servant; she is your best friend. She is not your old lady; she is your lover. She did not come from under your foot; she came from your side.

Sir, you ought never to be a demanding, self-absorbed, selfish, me-first kind of person. If you really want to have a great marriage, you will stop behaving as if you are entitled to this or that, and you will start behaving as if your highest goal is the welfare of your wife.

He had an attitude of self-glorification

Esther 1:3 *In the third year of his reign, he made a feast unto all his princes and his servants; the power of Persia and Media, the nobles and princes of the provinces, being before him:* **4** *When he shewed the riches of his* *glorious kingdom **and the honour of his excellent majesty** many days, even an hundred and fourscore days.*

It is almost hard to overstate just how arrogant this was. Ahasuerus threw a 180 day party for one main purpose, to show off! (Seven more days of partying were still to come.) This was a "pat Ahasuerus on the back party!"

There are male egos, and then there is stuff like this.

Now for starters, you single girls, this kind of thing usually does not start after marriage. It is usually pretty evident well before marriage. You may not see it, since you will be "twitterpated." But your daddy or mama will see it. So if they come to you and tell you that Cletus McDreamy is an arrogant little punk, break up with him.

But secondly, men, you who are married, some humility would do your marriage a lot of good. If you are more attracted to someone else than you are to your wife, it is going to cause a problem, especially if the person you are more attracted to is you!

I told my wife recently that I am going to start giving some unique marriage advice. I am going to start telling people that they need to break up with themselves. I see men, especially, that if they could go back and do it all over again, would probably take themselves to the prom, and then in their best Lionel Ritchie voice stand in the center of the dance floor and sing "I am so beautiful, to meee, can't you see, I'm everything I hoped for, everything I need, I am so beautiful, to me..."

Sir, if you want to be a marriage maker rather than a marriage breaker, you really ought to break up with yourself. An attitude of self-glorification will destroy a marriage.

He had an attitude of thoughtlessness
Esther 1:10 *On the seventh day, when the heart of the king was merry with wine, he commanded Mehuman, Biztha, Harbona, Bigtha, and Abagtha, Zethar, and Carcas,*

the seven chamberlains that served in the presence of Ahasuerus the king, 11 To bring Vashti the queen before the king with the crown royal, to shew the people and the princes her beauty: for she was fair to look on.

There are several evidences of his thoughtlessness to be found in these verses. The first evidence of his thoughtlessness is that he let alcohol cross his lips. Nothing good ever happens for a marriage by means of alcohol. A man does not become a better provider or a better spiritual leader or a better father or a better *anything* by drinking!

The second evidence of his thoughtlessness is that he sent other men to order his wife around.

You say, "But he was a king!" Yes, but his most important position was that of *husband*. You should know your Bible well enough to know that there is no position on earth that a man can hold that is more important than that of husband! A man is one flesh with his wife (Genesis 2:24) not with his kingdom or his church or his job or his children. I do not care what position you hold, sir, the most important role you hold is that of husband, and you better demonstrate thoughtfulness in that role!

Ladies, would you be offended if your husband sent other men to order you around? Yes! Men, this was just an evidence of his thoughtlessness.

The third evidence of his thoughtlessness is that he asked her to do something that she was not going to be comfortable doing. Surely I do not even have to ask this. Is there really any man who thinks that his wife would feel comfortable getting immodest in front of his drunken buddies?

Sir, a little thoughtfulness goes a long way in marriage. If you will make a habit of thinking through how your words or your actions are going to affect your wife *before* you say those words or do those actions, you may just save your marriage.

He had an attitude of unmanaged anger

Esther 1:12 *But the queen Vashti refused to come at the king's commandment by his chamberlains: therefore was **the king very wroth, and his anger burned in him**.*

Those words should paint a very clear picture of a man who had a bad temper and was regularly blowing his top. This was not an "odd slip" for Ahasuerus; history has recorded him as a man with anger issues.

When his army was marching toward Greece, a man named Pythius, who had given Xerxes a huge amount of money and supplies and to whom Xerxes had pledged undying friendship, asked a reasonable request. He had five sons, and all were in Xerxes army. He asked if just one of them could stay home, to take care of him and his wife in their old age. Xerxes flew into a rage. He agreed to leave that one son behind...in two pieces. He had his army cut the boy in half, and then marched his entire army between those two pieces as they left town with a father and mother left behind sobbing over their loss.

That does not begin to tell the full tale of his temper and cruelty, though. He also had the builders of the bridge over the Hellespont beheaded because a massive storm destroyed the bridge.

When he was in a storm out on the ocean and the storm was sinking his ships, he blew his stack so badly that he took his belt off and was beating the waves with it. Is it any surprise, then, that he blew his stack with his wife and destroyed his marriage? You ought to pay attention to what the Bible says about this matter of unmanaged anger:

Ecclesiastes 7:9 *Be not hasty in thy spirit to be angry: for anger resteth in the bosom of fools.*

Proverbs 22:24 *Make no friendship with an angry man; and with a furious man thou shalt not go:* **25** *Lest thou learn his ways, and get a snare to thy soul.*

Proverbs 29:22 *An angry man stirreth up strife, and a furious man aboundeth in transgression.*

Sir, you will either get a grip on your temper, or you will lose your grip on your marriage. And you can do it. People do what is important to them!

A few years ago a gentleman in our church was informed that he had diabetes. He has not put an ounce of sugar in his mouth since then; he did what was important to him.

A lady we are friends with raised her own kids, but recently took in her half a dozen grandkids and is raising them. She is doing what is important to her.

A couple we counseled years ago had more problems than you could count. They worked through them all. They did what was important to them.

Sir, you can do it if it is important to you, so get a grip on your temper before you lose your grip on your marriage!

He had an attitude of overreaction

Verse thirteen to the end of the chapter is so funny that it is sad, and so sad that it is funny. Look at it with me:

Esther 1:13 *Then the king said to the wise men, which knew the times, (for so was the king's manner toward all that knew law and judgment:* **14** *And the next unto him was Carshena, Shethar, Admatha, Tarshish, Meres, Marsena, and Memucan, the seven princes of Persia and Media, which saw the king's face, and which sat the first in the kingdom;)* **15** *What shall we do unto the queen Vashti according to law, because she hath not performed the commandment of the king Ahasuerus by the chamberlains?*

May I remind you, please, of the condition of these seven geniuses? All of them had now spent 187 days at the drinking party. They reeked of booze, their eyes were red, their speech was slurred, they were toasted. These were the men that the king turned to for guidance!

It takes a very foolish man to turn to drunken buddies for guidance on his marriage or anything else for that matter. It takes a foolish person, man or woman, to turn to any wrong person or persons for guidance.

People are thinking of getting out of church, so instead of going to someone who has been faithful for thirty years, they go ask the people who have all the stability of a rabid squirrel what they think.

A lady is thinking of leaving her husband, so she asks the woman at work who is on husband number five what she thinks.

Ahasuerus turned to his drunken hired hands and asked what they thought should be done. Predictably, he got an answer that only brain-dead drunks could ever come up with.

Esther 1:16 *And Memucan answered before the king and the princes, Vashti the queen hath not done wrong to the king only, but also to all the princes, and to all the people that are in all the provinces of the king Ahasuerus.* **17** *For this deed of the queen shall come abroad unto all women, so that they shall despise their husbands in their eyes, when it shall be reported, The king Ahasuerus commanded Vashti the queen to be brought in before him, but she came not.* **18** *Likewise shall the ladies of Persia and Media say this day unto all the king's princes, which have heard of the deed of the queen. Thus shall there arise too much contempt and wrath.* **19** *If it please the king, let there go a royal commandment from him, and let it be written among the laws of the Persians and the Medes, that it be not altered, That Vashti come no more before king Ahasuerus; and let the king give her royal estate unto another that is better than she.*

Notice, please, something that Memucan does as he begins to tell what should happen to Vashti. There is a word that he uses five times in three verses:

Esther 1:16 *And Memucan answered before the king and the princes, Vashti the queen hath not done wrong to the king only, but also to **all** the princes, and to **all** the people that are in **all** the provinces of the king Ahasuerus. **17** For this deed of the queen shall come abroad unto **all** women, so that they shall despise their husbands in their eyes, when it shall be reported, The king Ahasuerus commanded Vashti the queen to be brought in before him, but she came not. **18** Likewise shall the ladies of Persia and Media say this day unto **all** the king's princes, which have heard of the deed of the queen. Thus shall there arise too much contempt and wrath.*

May I paraphrase? "King, you gots ta do somethin. Every single woman in the whole wide world is gonna hear what Vashti did, and every one of those women in every country in the whole wide world is gonna git all high and mighty against their husbands!"

Do you think that perhaps that is just a bit melodramatic? It takes drunken men to come up with something so over the top as that. The truth is, if Ahasuerus had just let it go, it would have probably been forgotten. Everyone was drunk anyway! How much do you think they were going to remember about all of this once they sobered up? But by publishing it all around the world, which he literally did, everybody in the world did find out about it! The overreaction to the problem caused far more trouble than the problem itself.

Notice also, though, the self-serving rationale behind what Memucan said. According to verse fourteen, He himself was one of those "princes" that he spoke of whose wife was likely to "git all uppity" as verse eighteen says. He was not looking out for Ahasuerus, he was looking out for himself. Had Ahasuerus not been drunk, he would have been able to figure that out rather quickly.

These princes, led by Memucan, told Ahasuerus that he needed to divorce his wife, Vashti. Here is what he said:

Esther 1:19 *If it please the king, let there go a royal commandment from him, and let it be written among the laws of the Persians and the Medes, that it be not altered, That Vashti come no more before king Ahasuerus; and let the king give her royal estate unto another that is better than she. 20 And when the king's decree which he shall make shall be published throughout all his empire, (for it is great,) all the wives shall give to their husbands honour, both to great and small.*

What he said and suggested can be summed up this way, "I've got a great idea, King. Take your beautiful, spunky wife and divorce her. Then make a law that she can never be queen again. Then tell everybody in the entire world about it. That way, even though you'll be single and have to find another wife somehow, our wives will treat us better!"

It takes a drunken fool to suggest something like that, and it takes an even bigger drunken fool to go along with such an overreaction. But alas:

Esther 1:21 *And the saying pleased the king and the princes; and the king did according to the word of Memucan:*

No one there had enough sense to realize how ridiculous they were all being. They were *pleased* by the idea. Men, you that believe you have a beautiful wife, how pleased would you be to no longer have your beautiful wife? Somehow, Ahasuerus was pleased by this. Five minutes earlier she was the greatest thing on earth and so incredibly hot that he was willing to violate every law and custom of Persia to show her off, and now he is instantly ready to give her up forever. Overreaction, you think?

72

Esther 1:22 *For he sent letters into all the king's provinces, into every province according to the writing thereof, and to every people after their language, that every man should bear rule in his own house, and that it should be published according to the language of every people.*

As you read this verse, I am pretty certain I know what you are thinking if you know your Bible. You are thinking, "That actually sounds Biblical." You are partially correct. Look at Ephesians 5:

Ephesians 5:22 *Wives, submit yourselves unto your own husbands, as unto the Lord.* **23** *For the husband is the head of the wife, even as Christ is the head of the church: and he is the saviour of the body.* **24** *Therefore as the church is subject unto Christ, so let the wives be to their own husbands in every thing.*

Comparing those two passages, it sounds very much like the content is basically the same in both. And if you think that...you are correct, it is. Both of them basically say the same thing–that the man is to bear rule in his own home. But the message in Esther is a flawed message. You see, there are two ways a message can be flawed. It can be flawed in the content of the message, or it can be flawed in the character of the messenger. In Ephesians 5 we find husbands, who are supposed to bear rule in their own homes, being told to love their wives as Christ loved the church and to give themselves for their wives as Christ gave Himself for the church. But where do you find that in the message given by Ahasuerus in Esther? It is not there. These men were intent on having the authority, but they gave no thought at all to demonstrating love and sacrifice for their wives, and that is why they all, especially Ahasuerus, overreacted so badly.

If Ahasuerus would have loved his wife, this would never have even been an issue, because he would not have asked her to do something so wrong. It was a flawed message because he was a flawed messenger!

Men, take heed. Men who love their wives like Christ loved the church just about never have to even mention the command of Ephesians 5. I have been married for twenty years, and I have never had to remind my wife to submit to me, not once! I have made it my business to love her like crazy, and to treat her like royalty, and to sacrifice myself for her, and to put her first, and because of that, she lets me be in charge of the home without me ever having to ask for it or demand it.

But back to this thing of overreaction. Sir, you need to think of something very practical, and that is this: you cannot unring a bell. In other words, once you have overreacted, you cannot go back and undo it. But if you make a habit of underreacting, you can always escalate things later if you need to.

Men, love your wives enough to be in the habit of underreacting to any way that she gets under your skin. Your marriage is too important to destroy.

Ahasuerus did not destroy his home in any of the "usual" ways. He did not destroy it be cheating on her, he did not destroy it by abusing her, he did not destroy it by neglecting her, he destroyed it 100% by his bad attitude. Sir, I have a question for you. Would you be willing to give your daughter away in marriage to a young man who has an attitude just exactly like yours? If not, you have some work to do—work that needs to be done on your knees before the Lord.

Chapter 6
She Made Run Around Sue Look Like
Mother Theresa

"Well hello there, it is so good to see you tonight! My name really is not that important; it is not even mentioned in that book that you call the Bible. But even though my name is not mentioned, a lot is said about me, especially in one particular chapter. You can read it if you like, but I do not recommend it. I have read it, and it is clear to me that I have just been misunderstood.

"Maybe I should back up and tell you a few things about myself. For one, I am married. My husband is hard working, a good provider, all of that...stuff. But you know, a girl just needs more. He just does not understand me; that is the main problem. I just want to have a little fun, and he keeps expecting me to do things that are just unreasonable, like cook, and clean house, and be faithful to him! Who can live like that?

"I am repressed; that is the problem. But then, I know you understand that, you men, that is. None of you are like him. I can tell by looking at you, you are kind, and sweet, and romantic...all of the things my husband is not.

"Maybe you could come over for a while and we could...talk about it. My husband is out of town right now, so tonight would be good! Who am I, you ask? Well, the Bible just calls me 'The Strange Woman.'"

Proverbs 7:1 *My son, keep my words, and lay up my comman-dments with thee.* **2** *Keep my commandments, and live; and my law as the apple of thine eye.* **3** *Bind them upon thy fingers, write them upon the table of thine heart.* **4** *Say unto wisdom, Thou art my sister; and call understanding thy kinswoman:* **5** *That they may keep thee from the strange woman, from the stranger which flattereth with her words.* **6** *For at the window of my house I looked through my casement,* **7** *And beheld among the simple ones, I discerned among the youths, a young man void of understanding,* **8** *Passing through the street near her corner; and he went the way to her house,* **9** *In the twilight, in the evening, in the black and dark night:* **10** *And, behold, there met him a woman with the attire of an harlot, and subtil of heart.* **11** *(She is loud and stubborn; her feet abide not in her house:* **12** *Now is she without, now in the streets, and lieth in wait at every corner.)* **13** *So she caught him, and kissed him, and with an impudent face said unto him,* **14** *I have peace offerings with me; this day have I payed my vows.* **15** *Therefore came I forth to meet thee, diligently to seek thy face, and I have found thee.* **16** *I have decked my bed with coverings of tapestry, with carved works, with fine linen of Egypt.* **17** *I have perfumed my bed with myrrh, aloes, and cinnamon.* **18** *Come, let us take our fill of love until the morning: let us solace ourselves with loves.* **19** *For the goodman is not at home, he is gone a long journey:* **20** *He hath taken a bag of money with him, and will come home at the day appointed.* **21** *With her much fair speech she caused him to yield, with the flattering of her lips she forced him.* **22** *He goeth after her straightway, as an ox goeth to the slaughter, or as a fool to the correction of the stocks;* **23** *Till a dart strike through his liver; as a bird hasteth to the snare,* *and knoweth not that it is for his life.* **24** *Hearken unto me now therefore, O ye children, and attend to the words of my mouth.* **25** *Let not thine heart decline to her ways, go not astray in her paths.* **26** *For she hath cast down many wounded: yea, many strong men have been slain by her.* **27** *Her house is the way to hell, going down to the chambers of death.*

In Proverbs 7, Solomon showed a very worried side. I would guess that in his position of power and prosperity and peace he did not worry about much.

But Solomon had a son. One, and only one, that we know of. He also had some experience with women. Actually, he had a lot of experience, since he said "I Do" one thousand times!

Solomon had a lot of insight into women, and he also had one son that he hoped would turn out right. Therefore, in Proverbs 7, he wrote to warn Rehoboam about a particular type of woman, and he used one woman in particular to illustrate her. He did not use her name, he just called her "The Strange Woman." The reason he did that is because there were, and doubtless are, a whole bunch more like her.

When we read and study and preach this chapter, it is almost always from the same angle. We almost always look at it in reference to the fact that young men ought to be avoiding strange women. And that is, in fact, the main way that it is written. But may I point something out? There is a second legitimate angle from which to look at this passage, and that is the fact that this woman had a husband and a home, and she was behaving in a way that wrecks and ruins marriages! She was a marriage breaker, and there is much that we can learn from her.

This was a wife who refused to be a "home maker"

Proverbs 7:11 *(She is loud and stubborn; her feet abide not in her house:* **12** *Now is she without, now in the streets, and lieth in wait at every corner.)*

This is really where it all begins with her. This married woman had no use for home life. Her husband was merely a security blanket for her, a meal provider, someone to keep her up so she could run around and play with those who could not keep her up. She was a "liberated woman," one who would have detested and abhorred any June Cleaver type. She also would have loathed to read the words written by Paul to Titus.

Titus 2:3 *The aged women likewise, that they be in behaviour as becometh holiness, not false accusers, not given to much wine, teachers of good things;* **4** *That they may teach the young women to be sober, to love their husbands, to love their children,* **5** *To be discreet, chaste, keepers at home, good, obedient to their own husbands, that the word of God be not blasphemed.*

This passage would have sent the Strange Woman then, and every strange woman today, into an apoplectic fury!

Does a woman have to stay "barefoot and pregnant and in the kitchen?" No, the Proverbs 31 woman clearly did not! But, ladies, when you get married, your first priority and responsibility becomes to be a "keeper at home..."

If you still want to *act single,* then you need to *stay single.* Marriage comes with these great things called responsibilities.

I have seen some nasty homes where there was only a bachelor living there. But the nastiest homes I have ever seen were homes where there was a man and a wife and some kids and yet the wife still wanted to be a kid herself and would not stay home long enough to be a home maker!

78

This was a woman who dressed to impress men other than her husband

Proverbs 7:10 *And, behold, there met him a woman with the attire of an harlot, and subtil of heart.*

The Bible does not say that she was a harlot, it says that she dressed like one. Ma'am, you know how to dress in such a way that you look well-presented without drawing the undue attention of other men to your figure. And if you do dress to draw such attention, you know you are doing it, and you have a heart problem.

And mamas, you need to start early drawing the line on this with your own daughters. One of the most grievously inappropriate things to be seen in our modern society is the mother who intentionally dresses her daughter immodestly, or at least approves of and pays for that immodest style of dressing. Daughters used to have wonderful things called actual parents; I often wonder what has become of them!

The strange woman's habit of dressing to impress men other than her husband was a poisoning, devastating influence in that marriage.

This was a woman who had chosen to be "shameless"

Proverbs 7:13 *So she caught him, and kissed him, and with an **impudent** face said unto him,*

Impudent means bold, hard, unashamed. Get this. Think of what she was doing.

And think of the fact that she was utterly unembarrassed by it. She had seared her conscience, she had chosen to not be ashamed. Many years later the prophet Jeremiah would speak of this very type of thing:

Jeremiah 6:15 *Were they ashamed when they had committed abomination? nay, they were not at all ashamed, neither could they blush: therefore they shall fall among them that fall: at the time that I visit them they shall be cast down, saith the LORD.*

79

Ma'am, if you are doing something now that you would have been embarrassed by when you were actually right with the Lord, then you need to stop. And for the love of heaven, if you are living like the devil, would you please at least have enough decency not to drag God into your mess?

In our area there is a woman who abandoned her husband and multiple children to go and shack up with another man, who by the way was himself married! That is not the worst of it, though. The worst of it is that she is regularly on Facebook gushing over how much she loves the Lord and how blessed she is!

What she is, is a brazen harlot, a strange woman, and she is demonstrating it by choosing to be shameless over what should be humiliating to her!

This was a woman who was a religious hypocrite

Proverbs 7:13 *So she caught him, and kissed him, and with an impudent face said unto him,* **14** *I have peace offerings with me; this day have I payed my vows.* **15** *Therefore came I forth to meet thee, diligently to seek thy face, and I have found thee.*

Think of what she was saying to this man!

Matthew Henry put it this way: "She had been today at the temple, and was as well respected there as any that worshipped in the courts of the Lord. She had paid her vows, and, as she thought, made all even with God Almighty, and therefore might venture upon a new score of sins. Note, *The external performances of religion, if they do not harden men against sin, harden them in it*, and embolden carnal hearts to venture upon it, in hopes that when they come to count and discount with God he will be found as much in debt to them for their peace-offerings and their vows as they to him for their sins. But it is sad that a show of piety should become the shelter of iniquity (which really doubles the

80

shame of it, and makes it more exceedingly sinful) and that men should baffle their consciences with those very things that should startle them."

She was saying, "It is ok for you to commit adultery with me, I've been to church! I am a good girl, and it is ok to sin with good girls."

This woman was married, but was a religious hypocrite and because of that, she was destroying her marriage.

This was a woman who was not transparent with her husband

Proverbs 7:19 *For the goodman is not at home, he is gone a long journey: 20 He hath taken a bag of money with him, and will come home at the day appointed.*

He was gone, and she was keeping secrets. Wives, do not keep secrets from your husbands, do not even make him think you are keeping secrets. Transparency solves most every problem of jealousy!

This was a woman who could easily have had an incredible home life if she would have done for her husband what she did for other men

Proverbs 7:16 *I have decked my bed with coverings of tapestry, with carved works, with fine linen of Egypt. 17 I have perfumed my bed with myrrh, aloes, and cinnamon. 18 Come, let us take our fill of love until the morning: let us solace ourselves with loves.*

Look at what she did for another man! And the entire chapter is like this. If a woman like this would treat her husband like this she would have the marriage of the century. But sadly, many wives have already "conquered" their husband, and now they are looking for another conquest. They are taking the things that God has given them and using them for devilish purposes.

Proverbs 7:26 *For she hath cast down many wounded: yea, many strong men have been slain by her.*

This was not an isolated incident for this woman, it was a lifestyle. Her home was a disaster because of her behavior, and she ended up ruining countless other lives while in the process of destroying her own home.

Chapter 7
They Each Could Have Made It on Their Own, and that Is Why Their Marriage Was Such a Good One

"Greeting and salutations, and the Lord be with you!

"It is the distinct honor of me and my wife to speak with you by letter. We are both humbled to be included in your marriage study; there are doubtless so many couples more worthy than us!

"It is true, though, that we had a good marriage, even a great one. It was something, honestly, that neither of us expected. For my part, I had grown accustomed to the life of an older, eligible bachelor. I was a business man, and a very good one. My life was happy, I enjoyed my meals, each sunrise brought the possibilities of blessings in another brand new day.

"My wife, well, she was certainly from a very different background than me. I grew up knowing of the Lord, loving Him and serving Him. My wife had only in the last few years come to know Him. And that sets the stage for why I was so very taken with her. Despite a background of paganism, despite a legacy of sorrow and broken-heartedness, my dear wife was the most pleasant, joyful, happy person to be around!

"She was resourceful, this one. I believe that she would have continued to do fine even if we had never met. That thought by itself was enough to draw me to her and make me love her.

"Who are we? Why, we are the marriage in which each of us could have made it just fine on our own; we are Boaz and Ruth."

Ruth 4:9 *And Boaz said unto the elders, and unto all the people, Ye are witnesses this day, that I have bought all that was Elimelech's, and all that was Chilion's and Mahlon's, of the hand of Naomi.* **10** *Moreover Ruth the Moabitess, the wife of Mahlon, have I purchased to be my wife, to raise up the name of the dead upon his inheritance, that the name of the dead be not cut off from among his brethren, and from the gate of his place: ye are witnesses this day.* **11** *And all the people that were in the gate, and the elders, said, We are witnesses. The LORD make the woman that is come into thine house like Rachel and like Leah, which two did build the house of Israel: and do thou worthily in Ephratah, and be famous in Bethlehem:* **12** *And let thy house be like the house of Pharez, whom Tamar bare unto Judah, of the seed which the LORD shall give thee of this young woman.* **13** *So Boaz took Ruth, and she was his wife: and when he went in unto her, the LORD gave her conception, and she bare a son.*

This text gives us the account of the wedding of Boaz and Ruth and then of the fact that they produced a son together. Their story does not end there, though, not by a long shot.

Ruth 4:14 *And the women said unto Naomi, Blessed be the LORD, which hath not left thee this day without a kinsman, that his name may be famous in Israel.* **15** *And he shall be unto thee a restorer of thy life, and a nourisher of thine old age: for thy daughter in law, which loveth thee,* *which is better to thee than seven sons, hath born him.* **16** *And Naomi took the child, and laid it in her bosom, and became nurse unto it.* **17** *And the women her neighbours gave it a name, saying, There is a son born to Naomi; and they called his name Obed: he is the father of Jesse, the father of David.*

Boaz and Ruth became the great-grandparents of David, the greatest king the nation of Israel has ever had! But their story still does not end there.

Matthew 1:5 *And Salmon begat Booz of Rachab;* ***and Booz begat Obed of Ruth****; and Obed begat Jesse;* **6** *And Jesse begat David the king; and David the king begat Solomon of her that had been the wife of Urias;* **7** *And Solomon begat Roboam; and Roboam begat Abia; and Abia begat Asa;* **8** *And Asa begat Josaphat; and Josaphat begat Joram; and Joram begat Ozias;* **9** *And Ozias begat Joatham; and Joatham begat Achaz; and Achaz begat Ezekias;* **10** *And Ezekias begat Manasses; and Manasses begat Amon; and Amon begat Josias;* **11** *And Josias begat Jechonias and his brethren, about the time they were carried away to Babylon:* **12** *And after they were brought to Babylon, Jechonias begat Salathiel; and Salathiel begat Zorobabel;* **13** *And Zorobabel begat Abiud; and Abiud begat Eliakim; and Eliakim begat Azor;* **14** *And Azor begat Sadoc; and Sadoc begat Achim; and Achim begat Eliud;* **15** *And Eliud begat Eleazar; and Eleazar begat Matthan; and Matthan begat Jacob;* **16** *And Jacob begat Joseph the husband of Mary,* ***of whom was born Jesus, who is called Christ.***

Boaz and Ruth ended up as the great-grandparents of Jesus!

But their story really still does not even end there. Ruth has for 2,000 years been one of the most often preached from books in the Bible!

The book of Ruth has had books written about it, as far as I can tell, more than any other book in the Bible. This marriage was a great marriage, Boaz and Ruth were some real marriage makers! And one of the main secrets to that marriage success was something that may sound kind of odd. Each of them was quite capable of making it on their own and being happy on their own! Let's work our way through the book of Ruth and let me show you what I mean.

Ruth demonstrated the willingness to be without a husband if that is what it took to be right with God, and she had her convictions before she had a husband

Ruth 1:1 *Now it came to pass in the days when the judges ruled, that there was a famine in the land. And a certain man of Bethlehemjudah went to sojourn in the country of Moab, he, and his wife, and his two sons. 2 And the name of the man was Elimelech, and the name of his wife Naomi, and the name of his two sons Mahlon and Chilion, Ephrathites of Bethlehemjudah. And they came into the country of Moab, and continued there. 3 And Elimelech Naomi's husband died; and she was left, and her two sons. 4 And they took them wives of the women of Moab; the name of the one was Orpah, and the name of the other Ruth: and they dwelled there about ten years. 5 And Mahlon and Chilion died also both of them; and the woman was left of her two sons and her husband. 6 Then she arose with her daughters in law, that she might return from the country of Moab: for she had heard in the country of Moab how that the LORD had visited his people in giving them bread. 7 Wherefore she went forth out of the place where she was, and her two daughters in law with her; and they went on the way to return unto the land of Judah. 8 And Naomi said unto her two daughters in law, Go, return each to her mother's house: the LORD deal kindly with you, as ye have dealt with the dead, and with me. 9 The LORD grant you that ye may* *find rest, each of you in the house of her husband. Then she kissed them; and they lifted up their voice, and wept.* **10** *And they said unto her, Surely we will return with thee unto thy people.* **11** *And Naomi said, Turn again, my daughters: why will ye go with me? are there yet any more sons in my womb, that they may be your husbands?* **12** *Turn again, my daughters, go your way; for I am too old to have an husband. If I should say, I have hope, if I should have an husband also to night, and should also bear sons;* **13** *Would ye tarry for them till they were grown? would ye stay for them from having husbands? nay, my daughters; for it grieveth me much for your sakes that the hand of the LORD is gone out against me.* **14** *And they lifted up their voice, and wept again: and Orpah kissed her mother in law; but Ruth clave unto her.* **15** *And she said, Behold, thy sister in law is gone back unto her people, and unto her gods: return thou after thy sister in law.* **16** *And Ruth said, Intreat me not to leave thee, or to return from following after thee: for whither thou goest, I will go; and where thou lodgest, I will lodge: thy people shall be my people, and thy God my God:* **17** *Where thou diest, will I die, and there will I be buried: the LORD do so to me, and more also, if ought but death part thee and me.* **18** *When she saw that she was stedfastly minded to go with her, then she left speaking unto her.*

You who have been saved for many years probably know by now the basics of what was happening in this passage. But people who have not been saved that long are likely scratching their heads and wondering about all this because none of it is anything like the way that we do things now.

In our modern day, when a husband dies, the widow is free to go and marry whomever she chooses. My wife has already informed me that if I die, she is going to marry someone rich.

But in those days, the Jewish people were operating under a law and an expectation that came from that law. Naomi alluded to it. Here it is:

Deuteronomy 25:5 *If brethren dwell together, and one of them die, and have no child, the wife of the dead shall not marry without unto a stranger: her husband's brother shall go in unto her, and take her to him to wife, and perform the duty of an husband's brother unto her.* **6** *And it shall be, that the firstborn which she beareth shall succeed in the name of his brother which is dead, that his name be not put out of Israel.*

A woman married to a Jewish man understood that if he died she would be expected to wait for his brother (or some other near kinsman) to marry her. Ladies, that means that if you had lived back then, you would want to make sure that that dashingly handsome man you wanted to marry did not have a sniveling troll of a brother, just in case!

There were two young ladies in this bad position. It was not just Ruth; it was also her sister-in-law, Orpah. Both of them had a very clear choice before them–stay in Moab and marry a pagan Moabite, or go to Israel and stay single forever. Both of these girls had spent ten years in a Jewish home, both of them had heard the truth that Jehovah God was the only true God, and that the gods of the Moabites were not even real.

Look again at the choice they individually made:

Ruth 1:8 *And Naomi said unto her two daughters in law, Go, return each to her mother's house: the LORD deal kindly with you, as ye have dealt with the dead, and with me.* **9** *The LORD grant you that ye may find rest, each of you in the house of her husband. Then she kissed them; and they lifted up their voice, and wept.* **10** *And they said unto her, Surely we will return with thee unto thy people.* **11** *And Naomi said, Turn again, my daughters: why will ye go with me? are there yet any more sons in my womb, that they may* *be your husbands? 12 Turn again, my daughters, go your way; for I am too old to have an husband. If I should say, I have hope, if I should have an husband also to night, and should also bear sons; 13 Would ye tarry for them till they were grown? would ye stay for them from having husbands? nay, my daughters; for it grieveth me much for your sakes that the hand of the LORD is gone out against me. 14 And they lifted up their voice, and wept again: and Orpah kissed her mother in law; but Ruth clave unto her. 15 And she said, Behold, thy sister in law is gone back unto her people, and unto her gods: return thou after thy sister in law. 16 And Ruth said, Intreat me not to leave thee, or to return from following after thee: for whither thou goest, I will go; and where thou lodgest, I will lodge: thy people shall be my people, and thy God my God: 17 Where thou diest, will I die, and there will I be buried: the LORD do so to me, and more also, if ought but death part thee and me.*

Orpah weighed things out and made a choice. She decided that being right with God was not worth risking being single for the rest of her life, so she stayed in Moab.

Ruth also weighed things out and made a choice. She decided that being right with God was worth risking being single for the rest of her life, so she went to Israel.

What does this have to do with being a marriage maker? It has everything to do with it. Boaz ended up with a wife that he never had to doubt when it came to her spirituality. She had already made it very clear that she regarded being right with the Lord as being so important that if it was necessary she would be willing to stay single forever to do it! Ruth did not need a husband to be a godly woman; Ruth was a godly woman before she ever got a husband. Ruth did not need a husband to have convictions; she had convictions before she ever got a husband. Ruth did not need a husband to tell her what was right; she had already made up her mind about what was right before she ever got a husband. Man or woman, you who are single, this needs to be you. If you have to have a good spouse in order to do right, then you do not deserve a good spouse, and I am going to recommend to any potential ones that they avoid you!

I ministered to a down-and-out drunk many years ago. We spent many long hours riding in a car from place to place as I helped him hunt jobs, get power turned on, and many other things. I always used the time to talk to him about doing right. I remember a good many times when he would say, "Well if I had a good woman like yours, I could do right!"

And I would say, "No, if you would do right, you could have a good woman like mine!"

You need to make up your mind that being single is not the worst thing in the world. Being out of God's will is the worst thing in the world!

Let me put it another way. There is something worse than not having what you want, and that is having something that you do not want. If you are so weak spiritually that you are willing to marry an unsaved or unspiritual person just so that you will not have to be single, I can almost guarantee you that your marriage is going to be a disaster. Ruth and Boaz had a great marriage because Ruth demonstrated the willingness to be without a husband if that is what it took to be right with God, and she had her convictions before she had a husband.

Boaz was productive and successful while single

Ruth 2:1 *And Naomi had a kinsman of her husband's, a mighty man of wealth, of the family of Elimelech; and his name was Boaz.*

Boaz was single. Boaz did not have a wife. We do not know whether he was never married or whether his wife had died, but he was single. He was single, and he was a productive and successful businessman.

Men, Ruth did not have to "make him," he was already made. Ruth did not have to prod him to finish school, or prod him to find a job, or prod him to save for the future, or prod him to invest, Boaz was already doing all of that.

Let me give you a verse, please:

Proverbs 24:27 *Prepare thy work without, and make it fit for thyself in the field; and afterwards build thine house.*

That is exactly what Boaz did! Before there ever was a Ruth for him, he was already productive and successful. Now, yes, he was older, and no, it is not too likely that a person in their twenties will be rich by the time they get engaged. But the point is, men especially need to not be thinking, "When I get a wife, then I will focus on being productive and successful," they need to be thinking, "I am going to be productive and successful now, before I even get a wife."

You young men that are single, instead of spending all of your money on bows and guns and fishing rods and tickets to the game, why not put most of your money into stocks and bonds and money markets and a house and a good car and a savings account?

You really do not know if or when you will get married, but what you do know is that you cannot support a wife with bows and guns and fishing rods and ball game tickets. You cannot even support yourself with all of that.

The Wednesday night that I met Dana, once I finally convinced her to go out with me, I knew there were two things that I had going for me that any girl was definitely going to take note of. The first one was sitting in the parking lot. I had a new Honda sitting out there, a CRX, baby blue. I opened her door...tossed all of the random stuff into the back, and away we went in a vehicle that she knew was going to be reliable for years to come.

91

The second thing I let her see was a few miles down the road. I stopped at my little jewelry store that I owned, and went inside to get some cash to take her on the date with. I did not say anything about it, but there was my name, right on the window. She knew that I owned and operated my own business. May I tell you something? Casting out the line…nice juicy bait…strike!

A man ought not to flounder around until he gets a wife and then decide to make something of himself. No sir, you go make something of yourself now, so that some future wife will not have to do it for you! And the good part is, if you do make something of yourself and then you end up single for life, you can at least drown your loneliness in steak and lobster instead of beans and rice.

Ruth herself demonstrated that she could provide for herself without need of a man to do it for her

Ruth 2:2 *And Ruth the Moabitess said unto Naomi, Let me now go to the field, and glean ears of corn after him in whose sight I shall find grace. And she said unto her, Go, my daughter.* **3** *And she went, and came, and gleaned in the field after the reapers: and her hap was to light on a part of the field belonging unto Boaz, who was of the kindred of Elimelech.* **4** *And, behold, Boaz came from Bethlehem, and said unto the reapers, The LORD be with you. And they answered him, The LORD bless thee.* **5** *Then said Boaz unto his servant that was set over the reapers, Whose damsel is this?* **6** *And the servant that was set over the reapers answered and said, It is the Moabitish damsel that came back with Naomi out of the country of Moab:* **7** *And she said, I pray you, let me glean and gather after the reapers among the sheaves: so she came, and hath continued even from the morning until now, that she tarried a little in the house.*

May I summarize all of this? Ruth was smart enough and strong enough to provide for herself, thank you very much! She was smart enough to know the laws of the land that allowed her to go and work in the fields, and she was strong enough to do it and to do it all day long!

When it came to food on the table, Ruth did not need Boaz. She was allowed to go and work in any field she chose, and she was willing to do so. She was putting food on her own table. And that is one reason their marriage was such a great one–it was not a matter of need, it was a matter of want!

Ladies, hear me. Yes, a husband is commanded to provide for the family:

1 Timothy 5:8 *But if any provide not for his own, and specially for those of his own house, he hath denied the faith, and is worse than an infidel.*

But nowhere does the Bible forbid a woman from also being able to provide, first for herself alone and then later as a help to the husband if they both choose. The Proverbs 31 woman was an excellent contributor to the family finances. Acts 18:3 says that both Aquila and his wife, Priscilla, were tent makers, both of them. Ruth was an able and employed worker before she ever met Boaz.

Ladies, you who are single, prepare for your life as if you are going to need a career to feed yourself and others, prepare for your life as if there is not going to be anyone else there to provide for you. When I met Dana, she had a degree and two jobs. To this day she is smart enough and strong enough and capable enough that she does not *need* me to provide for her, she *allows* me to provide for her. And she also helps in that provision. Girls, get an education, learn a trade, have the ability to provide for yourselves. That way marriage becomes a matter of want, not of need.

And husbands, I am sure you are all excellent providers, but may I tell you something? You ought to never be afraid to allow your wife to become educated and capable of a career on her own. Why? Two reasons. One, you may

93

one day be dead, and she may be the one left to provide for herself and for your children. Two, you may one day be disabled, and she may need to provide for you! Boaz knew right off the bat that he was not just getting a pretty thing, he was also getting a woman with a good brain and the will to work.

Boaz did not need Ruth in order to be happy and satisfied with life; he was already happy and satisfied with life

     Ruth 3:1 *Then Naomi her mother in law said unto her, My daughter, shall I not seek rest for thee, that it may be well with thee? 2 And now is not Boaz of our kindred, with whose maidens thou wast? Behold, he winnoweth barley to night in the threshingfloor. 3 Wash thyself therefore, and anoint thee, and put thy raiment upon thee, and get thee down to the floor: but make not thyself known unto the man, until he shall have done eating and drinking. 4 And it shall be, when he lieth down, that thou shalt mark the place where he shall lie, and thou shalt go in, and uncover his feet, and lay thee down; and he will tell thee what thou shalt do. 5 And she said unto her, All that thou sayest unto me I will do. 6 And she went down unto the floor, and did according to all that her mother in law bade her. 7a And when Boaz had eaten and drunk, **and his heart was merry**...*

     Pay attention to this; it is very important. At this point in the text, did Boaz have any clue whatsoever that Ruth was even remotely interested in him? No, none at all. But the Bible says that "his heart was merry."

     Let me tell you what I have seen a lot of through the years. I have seen a lot of people that were so incredibly miserable that they did not have anybody, that their very misery kept them from ever getting anybody, which made them even more miserable, which made them even less likely to ever get anybody.

Years and years ago when I was maybe seven or eight, our church took a trip to Lake Lure. All the kids went swimming in the lake, and as one kid was walking up out of the lake, some girl pointed at him and screamed. He had these slimy looking creatures hanging all over him. They were leaches. They had attached themselves to him, and were doing their best to suck the life out of him. They had to be burned off of him.

You say, "Preacher, what does that have to do with this?" It has everything to do with it. A person who is emotionally dependent on someone else for their happiness is a human leach and will absolutely suck the life out of somebody.

How many of you at some point in your life were dating or courting somebody, and you came to the place where you realized that it needed to end, but when you tried to break it off that person said, "I'll kill myself if you dump me!"?

That is a human leach.

I know a man right now who is the most miserable human probably in the world, and his entire focus is on getting a wife. If he can just get a wife, he thinks he will be happy.

No, he will not. Someone else cannot carry you emotionally. You will drain the life out of them. The very best marriages are made up of two people who are already happy, and already living life to the fullest! The very best marriages are made up of people who walk with the Lord like He is their very closest friend.

We often deal with marriages that are having difficulties. One piece of advice that I almost always give to whomever is trying to make it work is to be happy. Live your life to the fullest whether your spouse ever comes home

95

or not. That way, you are an attractive person to come back to, and even if he/she does not come back, you are going to be fine because you have chosen to be happy anyway.

Men, ladies, if you search through the book of Ruth you will find that the only emotionally draining person, the only one who could not seem to be happy alone, was Naomi. Ruth and Boaz were happy before they even had a clue about each other.

I will never consent to any of my children marrying someone who is going to be miserable if they do not marry him/her. I want my kids to be able to walk through life with someone by their side, not carrying someone on their back.

I have been married for twenty years now as I write this book. I was happy and productive and grounded in my convictions before I ever got married. Dana was happy and productive and grounded in her convictions before we ever got married. Both of us were capable of making it on our own. Our marriage was not a union of one strong person and one weak person. Our marriage was not a union of one independent person and one dependent person. Our marriage was not a union of one person who was emotionally grounded and one person who was an emotional wreck. Our marriage was not a matter of need; it was a matter of want.

If you want your marriage to be everything that it can possibly be, you need to be a happy, strong, confident, grounded person. And you can be such a person even if you are a physical wreck! One of the greatest marriages I know is that of a friend of mine and his wife, and he has been in a wheelchair for over twenty years. But he is always smiling and enjoying life, he loves the Lord, he has made something of himself, and he is fun to be around.

He could have chosen to be depressed, dreary, sad, emotionally draining, but he has chosen to do the opposite, and his wife wants him!

You who are single, do not go looking for someone to make you happy. Be happy, and you will not have to look.

Chapter 8
The Marriage that Overcame the Odds

"Merry Christmas! We regard it as a joy to communicate with you by letter. Our marriage was perhaps the most unique of all times. One of the most problematic as well. Do you think you have problems in your marriage? Trust me; compared to us, your marriage is a stroll in the park. Name the problem, and we most likely had it. Poverty, suspicion, homelessness, slander, and even people trying to kill us!

"But despite all of the problems and difficulties, our marriage was a good one, a very good one. If you are a family with problems who would like to have a great home anyway, then we are the couple for you.

"Who are we? Why, we are the marriage that overcame the odds; we are Mary and Joseph!"

Matthew 1:18 *Now the birth of Jesus Christ was on this wise: When as his mother Mary was espoused to Joseph, before they came together, she was found with child of the Holy Ghost. 19 Then Joseph her husband, being a just man, and not willing to make her a publick example, was minded to put her away privily. 20 But while he thought on these things, behold, the angel of the Lord appeared unto him in a* *dream, saying, Joseph, thou son of David, fear not to take unto thee Mary thy wife: for that which is conceived in her is of the Holy Ghost.* **21** *And she shall bring forth a son, and thou shalt call his name JESUS: for he shall save his people from their sins.* **22** *Now all this was done, that it might be fulfilled which was spoken of the Lord by the prophet, saying,* **23** *Behold, a virgin shall be with child, and shall bring forth a son, and they shall call his name Emmanuel, which being interpreted is, God with us.* **24** *Then Joseph being raised from sleep did as the angel of the Lord had bidden him, and took unto him his wife:* **25** *And knew her not till she had brought forth her firstborn son: and he called his name JESUS.*

The circumstances in the marriage of Joseph and Mary were perfectly divine, but they were also potentially destructive. This marriage had perhaps more things lined up against it than any other marriage ever, yet Joseph and Mary were marriage makers, and they made a good one.

Let's find out how.

The worth of the marriage

Matthew 13:55 *Is not this the carpenter's son? is not his mother called Mary? and his brethren, James, and Joses, and Simon, and Judas?* **56** *And his sisters, are they not all with us? Whence then hath this man all these things?*

What we read in these verses occurred more than thirty years after the miraculous night of Mary's conception. Despite all of the things working against them, Mary and Joseph stayed together. In fact, they had a good enough relationship to produce at least six other children together! These were two that truly valued their marriage; it was of infinite worth to them.

This is exactly how every marriage should be viewed by the husband and wife within it. Despite the modern culture's laissez faire attitude toward marriage, the husband

and wife with any wisdom at all will view marriage as something to fight for, pray over, sacrifice to make better, and cherish above all else.

The warfare against the marriage

Mary and Joseph really did have the deck stacked against them. If you think that you have it hard in your marriage, consider what they were facing.

Suspicion:

Matthew 1:18 *Now the birth of Jesus Christ was on this wise: When as his mother Mary was espoused to Joseph, before they came together, she was found with child of the Holy Ghost.* **19** *Then Joseph her husband, being a just man, and not willing to make her a publick example, was minded to put her away privily.*

Joseph thought the same thing any man today would think if his fiancé turned up pregnant! And that suspicion caused him to make plans to end the marriage.

Poor planning:

Luke 2:1 *And it came to pass in those days, that there went out a decree from Caesar Augustus, that all the world should be taxed.* **2** *(And this taxing was first made when Cyrenius was governor of Syria.)* **3** *And all went to be taxed, every one into his own city.* **4** *And Joseph also went up from Galilee, out of the city of Nazareth, into Judaea, unto the city of David, which is called Bethlehem; (because he was of the house and lineage of David:)* **5** *To be taxed with Mary his espoused wife, being great with child.*

Every Jew knew the Old Testament, and thus knew that the prophet Micah had foretold that Bethlehem must be the birthplace of the Messiah. That being the case, Mary and Joseph had many months to travel from Nazareth to Bethlehem. The trip should have only taken them a few days. Yet right before she was to give birth, they had to make a hurried trip to Bethlehem, and even then they only went because of the decree of Caesar Augustus! This was clearly a case of poor planning, and poor planning can place a heavy strain on any marriage.

Poverty:

Luke 2:21 *And when eight days were accomplished for the circumcising of the child, his name was called JESUS, which was so named of the angel before he was conceived in the womb.* **22** *And when the days of her purification according to the law of Moses were accomplished, they brought him to Jerusalem, to present him to the Lord;* **23** *(As it is written in the law of the Lord, Every male that openeth the womb shall be called holy to the Lord;)* **24** *And to offer a sacrifice according to that which is said in the law of the Lord, A pair of turtledoves, or two young pigeons.*

Leviticus 12:8 tells us that people who were not able to afford a lamb for the sacrifice could bring the two specified birds instead. The fact that Mary and Joseph did so is an indication of their poverty. You who are, or at one point have been, struggling financially know the strain this can put on a marriage!

Unexpected problems:

Matthew 2:1 *Now when Jesus was born in Bethlehem of Judaea in the days of Herod the king, behold, there came wise men from the east to Jerusalem,* **2** *Saying, Where is he that is born King of the Jews? for we have seen his star in the east, and are come to worship him.* **3** *When Herod the king had heard these things, he was troubled, and all Jerusalem with him.* **4** *And when he had gathered all the chief priests and scribes of the people together, he demanded of them where Christ should be born.* **5** *And they said unto him, In Bethlehem of Judaea: for thus it is written by the prophet,* **6** *And thou Bethlehem, in the land of Juda, art not the least among the princes of Juda: for out of thee shall come a Governor, that shall rule my people Israel.* **7** *Then*

Herod, when he had privily called the wise men, enquired of them diligently what time the star appeared. 8 And he sent them to Bethlehem, and said, Go and search diligently for the young child; and when ye have found him, bring me word again, that I may come and worship him also. 9 When they had heard the king, they departed; and, lo, the star, which they saw in the east, went before them, till it came and stood over where the young child was. 10 When they saw the star, they rejoiced with exceeding great joy. 11 And when they were come into the house, they saw the young child with Mary his mother, and fell down, and worshipped him: and when they had opened their treasures, they presented unto him gifts; gold, and frankincense, and myrrh. 12 And being warned of God in a dream that they should not return to Herod, they departed into their own country another way. 13 And when they were departed, behold, the angel of the Lord appeareth to Joseph in a dream, saying, Arise, and take the young child and his mother, and flee into Egypt, and be thou there until I bring thee word: for Herod will seek the young child to destroy him. 14 When he arose, he took the young child and his mother by night, and departed into Egypt:

There is not much chance that Mary and Joseph expected any of this! How could they know that they were going to be in the middle of a mass murder aimed at their son, and that they would have to run for their lives into a foreign country? Though these things were prophesied in the Old Testament, it was not until after they had happened that they were able to be clearly understood. Problems are hard enough on a marriage, but unexpected problems are far worse!

Outside interference:

John 8:41 *Ye do the deeds of your father. Then said they to him, We be not born of fornication; we have one Father, even God.*

The words spoken here were spoken thirty years or more after the birth of Christ. In other words, for their entire marriage Mary and Joseph were being bothered by outsiders saying things about them that were not true. That had to be hard on the marriage!

The pressure of a growing family:

Matthew 13:55 *Is not this the carpenter's son? is not his mother called Mary? and his brethren, James, and Joses, and Simon, and Judas?*

Thinking of the list of difficulties they were already facing, how much more must all of them have been magnified by the fact that they had such a rapidly growing family! All of these things put together would seem to be a death knell for any marriage. But Mary and Joseph made their marriage work in spite of all the things they had lined up against them. That being the case, there is clearly much we can learn from them! So how did they do it?

The way they made the marriage

By keeping their problems private:

Matthew 1:19 *Then Joseph her husband, being a just man, and not willing to make her a publick example, was minded to put her away privily.*

From the very earliest days of their relationship Mary and Joseph got one major thing very, very right–they kept their problems private! There is no problem so bad that it cannot be made worse by being made public. Husbands, wives, keep your problems off of Facebook, Twitter, out of the workplace, and out of the earshot of anyone who isn't you! The only exception should be when you need to see your pastor for counseling. Other than that, circle the family wagons and keep your marital problems private!

By making "doing right" the most important consideration at all times:

Matthew 1:20 *But while he thought on these things, behold, the angel of the Lord appeared unto him in a dream, saying, Joseph, thou son of David, fear not to take unto thee Mary thy wife: for that which is conceived in her is of the Holy Ghost.* **21** *And she shall bring forth a son, and thou shalt call his name JESUS: for he shall save his people from their sins.* **22** *Now all this was done, that it might be fulfilled which was spoken of the Lord by the prophet, saying,* **23** *Behold, a virgin shall be with child, and shall bring forth a son, and they shall call his name Emmanuel, which being interpreted is, God with us.* **24** *Then Joseph being raised from sleep did as the angel of the Lord had bidden him, and took unto him his wife:*

It would have been much easier for Joseph to do the exact opposite of what he was asked to do. Joseph knew full well that, if he obeyed God's wishes on this, he was letting himself in for a lifetime of trouble. But for Joseph, doing what was right was the most important consideration. This should also be the most important consideration for every husband and every wife today! A husband and wife who are intent on doing right will end up as marriage makers rather than marriage breakers.

By both maintaining the same high spiritual level:

Luke 1:26 *And in the sixth month the angel Gabriel was sent from God unto a city of Galilee, named Nazareth,* **27** *To a virgin espoused to a man whose name was Joseph, of the house of David; and the virgin's name was Mary.* **28** *And the angel came in unto her, and said, Hail, thou that art highly favoured, the Lord is with thee: blessed art thou among women.* **29** *And when she saw him, she was troubled at his saying, and cast in her mind what manner of salutation this should be.* **30** *And the angel said unto her, Fear not, Mary: for thou hast found favour with God.*

Matthew 1:20 *But while he thought on these things, behold, the angel of the Lord appeared unto him in a dream,*

105

saying, Joseph, thou son of David, fear not to take unto thee Mary thy wife: for that which is conceived in her is of the Holy Ghost. **21** *And she shall bring forth a son, and thou shalt call his name JESUS: for he shall save his people from their sins.* **22** *Now all this was done, that it might be fulfilled which was spoken of the Lord by the prophet, saying,* **23** *Behold, a virgin shall be with child, and shall bring forth a son, and they shall call his name Emmanuel, which being interpreted is, God with us.*

It is clear from both of these texts that both Mary and Joseph maintained a high spiritual level in their lives. Both were visited by angels. Both were in the habit of doing right. When either a husband or wife lags behind their spouse in spiritual matters, it damages the relationship. The strongest homes are those in which both the husband and wife maintain a good relationship with the Lord.

By being patient when it came to their own desires:

Matthew 1:24 *Then Joseph being raised from sleep did as the angel of the Lord had bidden him, and took unto him his wife:* **25** *And knew her not till she had brought forth her firstborn son: and he called his name JESUS.*

We often think the people in the Bible were spiritual giants. That is simply not the case. Joseph was a man like any other man. He had a natural desire for intimacy with his wife. Yet, in obedience to the Lord, he married his wife and was not intimate with her until after Jesus had been born. That is some excellent self-control and patience! No wonder Joseph was such a good husband and no wonder they had such a good marriage!

By Joseph fulfilling his responsibility as the head of the home:

Matthew 2:13 *And when they were departed, behold, the angel of the Lord appeareth to Joseph in a dream, saying, Arise, and take the young child and his mother, and flee into Egypt, and be thou there until I bring* *thee word: for Herod will seek the young child to destroy him.* **14** *When he arose, he took the young child and his mother by night, and departed into Egypt:* **15** *And was there until the death of Herod: that it might be fulfilled which was spoken of the Lord by the prophet, saying, Out of Egypt have I called my son.*

Matthew 2:19 *But when Herod was dead, behold, an angel of the Lord appeareth in a dream to Joseph in Egypt,* **20** *Saying, Arise, and take the young child and his mother, and go into the land of Israel: for they are dead which sought the young child's life.* **21** *And he arose, and took the young child and his mother, and came into the land of Israel.*

The picture painted of this home by the Roman Catholic Church would show Mary in charge and Joseph as being of little significance. But God designed the home with the man as that head, and the home of Mary and Joseph was no different. When trouble came, God came to Joseph to tell him what to do. Mary was blessed with a very good husband in Joseph. He took his responsibility as head of the home seriously, and he did a good job of it.

By staying in "church:"

Luke 2:42 *And when he was twelve years old, they went up to Jerusalem after the custom of the feast.* **43** *And when they had fulfilled the days, as they returned, the child Jesus tarried behind in Jerusalem; and Joseph and his mother knew not of it.* **44** *But they, supposing him to have been in the company, went a day's journey; and they sought him among their kinsfolk and acquaintance.* **45** *And when they found him not, they turned back again to Jerusalem, seeking him.* **46** *And it came to pass, that after three days they found him in the temple, sitting in the midst of the doctors, both hearing them, and asking them questions.* **47** *And all that heard him were astonished at his understanding and answers.*

107

If there was ever a home that was blessed enough and spiritual enough not to need to go to the house of the Lord you would think the home of Mary and Joseph would be it! After all, they literally had the Son of God living with them! But here they were twelve years later still being faithful to attend the house of the Lord. A marriage that is faithful to church, and I do not mean just sort of faithful, I mean really faithful to church, is likely to be a very good strong marriage! When troubles come to the home one of the first things people want to do is get out of church. Unfortunately, that is one of the worst things anybody can do. If you want a really good strong marriage that is blessed by God and is likely to last, please know that it will not happen if you decide to be unfaithful to the house of God.

By Mary promoting Joseph:

Luke 2:48 *And when they saw him, they were amazed: and his mother said unto him, Son, why hast thou thus dealt with us? behold, thy father and I have sought thee sorrowing.* **49** *And he said unto them, How is it that ye sought me? wist ye not that I must be about my Father's business?*

Mary was not perfect. In these verses she made a mistake. She referred to Joseph as the father of Jesus. Joseph was not the father of Jesus. But in spite of the fact that she made that mistake, there is a very large silver lining to be found within it. Mary was looking to her husband and promoting her husband! A wife who does that is likely to produce a very confident strong husband and thereby a very good marriage. If a wife has to make a mistake one way or the other, she would do much better to make a mistake promoting her husband than denigrating her husband!

By both of them enjoying each other, a lot:

Matthew 13:55 *Is not this the carpenter's son? is not his mother called Mary? and his brethren, James, and Joses,* *and Simon, and Judas?* **56** *And his sisters, are they not all with us? Whence then hath this man all these things?*

Without trying to be the least bit crass or base, may I point out that for the man at least, there are very few problems that cannot be solved by a trip to the bedroom! I am sure Joseph was in the carpentry shop quite a lot, and I am sure that Mary was the kitchen quite a lot, but it is evident from these verses that they were also both in the bedroom quite a lot! This is a natural God-given desire, it draws a man and his wife closer together, and it is clearly one of the reasons that Mary and Joseph were marriage makers rather than marriage breakers.

Chapter 9
The Couple that Was Forged by Fire

"Greetings, fellow lovers of the Lord and of life. Please forgive the spots on the paper as I write. I struggle these days to keep dry eyes as I think back on all that my dear wife and I have gone through. Mind you, these are not entirely tears of sadness. In fact, I would say that a great many of them are actually tears of gratitude. Given all that I–that my wife and I–lost, the fact that we are still together means more to me than anyone can imagine. The fires burned long and hot in our lives, and there were a great many times that I was certain that it would consume us both. In fact, there are many times I actually wished that it would.

"But, after it all, here we still are! The fires that burned turned out to be the fires of a forge, not the fires of destruction. What my wife and I had was strengthened by that which Satan intended for our destruction.

"Are you perchance hurting? Does it seem like the circumstances of life are going to wreck and ruin your marriage? Then I suggest you pay very close attention to our story. Who are we? Why, we are the couple that was forged by the fire; we are Mr. and Mrs. Job."

Job 1:1 *There was a man in the land of Uz, whose name was Job; and that man was perfect and upright, and*

111

*one that feared God, and eschewed evil. **2** And there were born unto him seven sons and three daughters. **3** His substance also was seven thousand sheep, and three thousand camels, and five hundred yoke of oxen, and five hundred she asses, and a very great household; so that this man was the greatest of all the men of the east. **4** And his sons went and feasted in their houses, every one his day; and sent and called for their three sisters to eat and to drink with them. **5** And it was so, when the days of their feasting were gone about, that Job sent and sanctified them, and rose up early in the morning, and offered burnt offerings according to the number of them all: for Job said, It may be that my sons have sinned, and cursed God in their hearts. Thus did Job continually. **6** Now there was a day when the sons of God came to present themselves before the LORD, and Satan came also among them. **7** And the LORD said unto Satan, Whence comest thou? Then Satan answered the LORD, and said, From going to and fro in the earth, and from walking up and down in it. **8** And the LORD said unto Satan, Hast thou considered my servant Job, that there is none like him in the earth, a perfect and an upright man, one that feareth God, and escheweth evil? **9** Then Satan answered the LORD, and said, Doth Job fear God for nought? **10** Hast not thou made an hedge about him, and about his house, and about all that he hath on every side? thou hast blessed the work of his hands, and his substance is increased in the land. **11** But put forth thine hand now, and touch all that he hath, and he will curse thee to thy face. **12** And the LORD said unto Satan, Behold, all that he hath is in thy power; only upon himself put not forth thine hand. So Satan went forth from the presence of the LORD. **13** And there was a day when his sons and his daughters were eating and drinking wine in their eldest brother's house: **14** And there came a messenger unto Job, and said, The oxen were plowing, and the asses feeding beside them: **15** And the*

Sabeans fell upon them, and took them away; yea, they have slain the servants with the edge of the sword; and I only am escaped alone to tell thee. **16** *While he was yet speaking, there came also another, and said, The fire of God is fallen from heaven, and hath burned up the sheep, and the servants, and consumed them; and I only am escaped alone to tell thee.* **17** *While he was yet speaking, there came also another, and said, The Chaldeans made out three bands, and fell upon the camels, and have carried them away, yea, and slain the servants with the edge of the sword; and I only am escaped alone to tell thee.* **18** *While he was yet speaking, there came also another, and said, Thy sons and thy daughters were eating and drinking wine in their eldest brother's house:* **19** *And, behold, there came a great wind from the wilderness, and smote the four corners of the house, and it fell upon the young men, and they are dead; and I only am escaped alone to tell thee.* **20** *Then Job arose, and rent his mantle, and shaved his head, and fell down upon the ground, and worshipped,* **21** *And said, Naked came I out of my mother's womb, and naked shall I return thither: the LORD gave, and the LORD hath taken away; blessed be the name of the LORD.* **22** *In all this Job sinned not, nor charged God foolishly.*

Job 2:1 *Again there was a day when the sons of God came to present themselves before the LORD, and Satan came also among them to present himself before the LORD.* **2** *And the LORD said unto Satan, From whence comest thou? And Satan answered the LORD, and said, From going to and fro in the earth, and from walking up and down in it.* **3** *And the LORD said unto Satan, Hast thou considered my servant Job, that there is none like him in the earth, a perfect and an upright man, one that feareth God, and escheweth evil? and still he holdeth fast his integrity, although thou movedst me against him, to destroy him without cause.* **4** *And Satan answered the LORD, and said, Skin for skin, yea, all* *that a man hath will he give for his life.* **5** *But put forth thine hand now, and touch his bone and his flesh, and he will curse thee to thy face.* **6** *And the LORD said unto Satan, Behold, he is in thine hand; but save his life.* **7** *So went Satan forth from the presence of the LORD, and smote Job with sore boils from the sole of his foot unto his crown.* **8** *And he took him a potsherd to scrape himself withal; and he sat down among the ashes.* **9** *Then said his wife unto him, Dost thou still retain thine integrity? curse God, and die.* **10** *But he said unto her, Thou speakest as one of the foolish women speaketh. What? shall we receive good at the hand of God, and shall we not receive evil? In all this did not Job sin with his lips.*

The trial of Job

Other than the Lord Jesus Christ, there has never been another person to suffer the way that Job suffered. Job was a wealthy man, a successful man, a man with a wife and several children.

But Job was also a man with an enemy. Unbeknownst to Job, the devil had been watching him very carefully. The Bible tells us that there was a day when the sons of God came to present themselves before the Lord, and Satan came also among them. God spoke to Satan and asked him what he had been doing. The devil replied that he had been going up and down to and fro in the earth. God then asked him if he had considered His servant Job.

Boy, had he ever!

The devil knew Job quite well. He began to accuse Job before God. The main thrust of his accusation was that Job was only serving God for profit and for the blessings that God gave.

So God basically said that Satan could take everything Job had but not to touch him.

In a matter of moments, Job lost it all. All of his possessions, all of his wealth, but worst of all, all of his children. And yet, the Bible tells us that in all this Job did not sin with his mouth or charge God foolishly.

But that was only round one. Sometime later Satan came again before the Lord and again leveled accusations at Job. This time he told God that as long as Job was healthy he would serve God, but if God ever allowed him to become unhealthy or in pain he would stop serving God, in fact he would curse God to his face.

So God lowered the protective barrier around Job even farther. He allowed the devil to do anything he wanted short of killing Job. Soon Job was covered with painful boils from the top of his head to the bottom of his feet. Every waking moment was painful, every sleeping moment was painful. It was so bad that Job began to regret that he had ever been born.

The toll on the marriage

Since the name of this book is the book of Job, it is easy to forget that there was a Mrs. Job as well. She went through everything that he went through, except for the attack on his body. This was a grieving mother who had lost her ten children. The devil was not able to get Job to curse God, but whether he intended to or not, he made things so bad that the marriage of Mr. and Mrs. Job begin to fray.

The first indication we have of this is her snapping at him.

Job 2:9 *Then said his wife unto him, Dost thou still retain thine integrity? curse God, and die.*

I am going to give her the benefit of the doubt on this. They had already had ten kids together, so I doubt seriously if this was a regular occurrence with her. But regular occurrence or not, Mrs. Job blew a gasket at her husband.

115

Then there was a distance between them.

Job 19:17 *My breath is strange to my wife, though I intreated for the children's sake of mine own body.*

The beginning and the end part of the book of Job is very famous and very well known. Lesser-known is all that took place within the middle of it. Job's three friends started a pretty nasty argument with him. In the midst of the book and in the midst of that argument Job said something that let us know how things were going in his marriage at that point.

It wasn't going well.

A distance had developed. Job's wife did not even want to be near him; she had no desire to help him no matter how badly he was hurting.

Their marriage was about one thin thread away from failing.

The triumph of a marriage maker

Things ended very well, when by all rights it seems that it should not have. Look at how the story ended:

Job 42:10 *And the LORD turned the captivity of Job, when he prayed for his friends: also the LORD gave Job twice as much as he had before. 11 Then came there unto him all his brethren, and all his sisters, and all they that had been of his acquaintance before, and did eat bread with him in his house: and they bemoaned him, and comforted him over all the evil that the LORD had brought upon him: every man also gave him a piece of money, and every one an earring of gold. 12 So the LORD blessed the latter end of Job more than his beginning: for he had fourteen thousand sheep, and six thousand camels, and a thousand yoke of oxen, and a thousand she asses. 13 He had also seven sons and three daughters. 14 And he called the name of the first, Jemima; and the name of the second, Kezia; and the name of the third, Kerenhappuch. 15 And in all the land were no women found so fair as the daughters of Job: and their* *father gave them inheritance among their brethren.* **16** *After this lived Job an hundred and forty years, and saw his sons, and his sons' sons, even four generations.* **17** *So Job died, being old and full of days.*

Job and his wife made it! Their marriage not only survived, it thrived.

How did this happen? This is really important, because the things that Job did will work in good times or bad. Let me remind you of something before we find out what he did:

Job 1:1 *There was a man in the land of Uz, whose name was Job; and that man was perfect and upright, and one that feared God, and eschewed evil.*

Job 2:3 *And the LORD said unto Satan, Hast thou considered my servant Job, that there is none like him in the earth, a perfect and an upright man, one that feareth God, and escheweth evil? and still he holdeth fast his integrity, although thou movedst me against him, to destroy him without cause.*

Job was right, and right with God. Keep that in mind. Here is what this marriage maker husband did.

Whether in prosperity or poverty or pain, Job maintained a godly walk:

It really is very easy to walk with the Lord and do right when everything is going well. But for Job, a godly walk was an all day every day thing whether in prosperity or poverty or pain. A husband like that is a marriage maker!

When the head of the home does not do right, the marriage is at risk. You, sir, are supposed to be a spiritual rock.

Proverbs 20:6 *Most men will proclaim every one his own goodness: but a faithful man who can find?*

That verse asked the question *a faithful man who can find?* Mrs. Job found one and she married him and that is

117

one of the reasons their marriage made it through the trials they faced.

Job was a real man for his wife and *to* his wife:

Job 2:9 *Then said his wife unto him, Dost thou still retain thine integrity? curse God, and die.* **10** *But he said unto her,* **Thou speakest as one of the foolish women speaketh***. What? shall we receive good at the hand of God, and shall we not receive evil? In all this did not Job sin with his lips.*

I want you to think of how hard this was for Job. As if he was not going through enough, his wife blew up, and he had to confront her over it. He was weak, he was hurting, he was sick, but he did not let any of those things stop him from being a real man for his wife and *to* his wife

Sir, never make it necessary for a pastor or any other man to confront your wife when she does wrong. It is not their job; it is your job. If you will not do so, eventually your weakness may destroy your own home.

This is the hardest thing for any man to ever have to do, but it needs to be done. Sir, love your wife enough to confront her when she is wrong even if that confrontation needs to take place publicly. I guarantee you that after this event Mrs. Job never doubted for a moment that she had married a real man!

Men, you are the spiritual head of your home, and you have just as much responsibility to spiritually shape your wife as you do your children!

Ephesians 5:23 *For the husband is the head of the wife, even as Christ is the head of the church: and he is the saviour of the body.*

There are certain things that the Bible is very clear on concerning men, but there are also certain things that the Bible is very clear on concerning ladies:

Proverbs 9:13 *A foolish woman is clamorous: she is simple, and knoweth nothing.*

Do you know what that word clamorous means? It means roaring, raging, making a noise, being loud, being in an uproar. The Bible says that it is not a good woman, not a wise woman, not a godly woman, it is foolish woman that is like that. What did Job say to his wife?

Thou speakest as one of the foolish women speaketh.

Look at these verses:

Proverbs 12:4 *A virtuous woman is a crown to her husband: but she that maketh ashamed is as rottenness in his bones.*

Proverbs 21:9 *It is better to dwell in a corner of the housetop, than with a brawling woman in a wide house.*

Proverbs 21:19 *It is better to dwell in the wilderness, than with a contentious and an angry woman.*

Proverbs 25:24 *It is better to dwell in the corner of the housetop, than with a brawling woman and in a wide house.*

Proverbs 27:15 *A continual dropping in a very rainy day and a contentious woman are alike.*

God is not at all pleased with a brawling, contentious woman. And whose job is it to make sure that does not happen? According to a perfect and upright husband named Job, it is the husband's job. According to Paul in Ephesians 5, it is the husband's job.

A few years ago, I was talking to a good pastor friend of mine and his wife, and they told me about the day a woman caused a screaming scene in church. Everyone looked back at her husband...and he shrugged! They are now gone, their kids are still there, and the kids do not even want their mother to come back! Daddy was afraid to do his job, and his wife is now firmly in place as the head of the home.

Listen to me, what Job was going through was a spiritual attack, and his wife knew what she was talking about. If he had listened to her, he would have been dead, which by extension would have destroyed their marriage. The only hope for Job to save his marriage was to confront his wife over her words and attitude.

Do you think that was easy? Of course not. But it was right, and doing it made Job a marriage maker. If we could put it in modern terms, Job "put on his big boy britches." He was not mean, he was not hateful, but he corrected her when she needed it. Mrs. Job had the best thing that any woman could ever have–a real man for a husband.

Job was steady, clearly in things for the long haul:

Job 1:1 *There was a man in the land of Uz, whose name was Job; and that man was perfect and upright, and one that feared God, and eschewed evil.* 2 ***And there were born unto him seven sons and three daughters.***

Job 42:12 *So the LORD blessed the latter end of Job more than his beginning: for he had fourteen thousand sheep, and six thousand camels, and a thousand yoke of oxen, and a thousand she asses.* 13 ***He had also seven sons and three daughters.***

Job was with his wife long enough to produce ten children and see them grow to adulthood...

Then they had the disaster...

Job stayed steady throughout the disaster...

Then he was with her long enough to produce ten more children!

Men, if you want to be a marriage maker, you better be a very steady kind of a person.

Mrs. Job would have changed a lot in her looks during this time...but he stayed steady.

Mrs. Job would have changed a lot in her emotional state during and after the disaster...but he stayed steady.

Job and his wife had to start all over on building a family and raising the kids (Their others were already raised!) yet Job stayed steady.

Their marriage survived because he just kept staying steady!

One of the godliest men I ever knew was B. L. Queen. He lost three children in the most dramatic and devastating ways possible. Yet through it all he stayed as steady as a rock for the Lord and for his wife. They overcame the tragic deaths of three children and served the Lord together as man and wife until way up in their eighties. There is something to be said for just staying steady!

Job, a man who was willing to correct his own wife when she was wrong, was also willing to cater to her when she was right:

Job 42:13 *He had also seven sons and three daughters.* **14** *And he called the name of the first, Jemima* **(Day)**; *and the name of the second, Kezia* **(A sweet smelling spice)**; *and the name of the third, Kerenhappuch* **(horn of plenty, figuratively "all I need".)** **15** *And in all the land were no women found so fair as the daughters of Job: and their father gave them inheritance among their brethren.*

Job paid special attention to his daughters. He named his daughters. He gave his daughters part of the inheritance. This was as much for his wife as for them! Mama had already lost her three daughters, and mothers and daughters get close. When she had three more, Job took time to care for his wife by doing special things for them. Fathers in those days usually cared only for sons!

Men, you better be willing to make her unhappy when she needs to be made unhappy, and happy when she needs to be happy!

Marriages can survive and thrive, even through the midst of terrible tragedy. Husbands, if you will do right, the fire will be a forge to strengthen your marriage rather than a force to destroy it.

Chapter 10
The Man Who Could Have Lived Without Her, but Couldn't Live Without Her

"May the Lord be with you, children of our Creator!

"As I look down from heaven and see what has become of the sons and daughters of men, I realize afresh and anew just how blessed I was in my marriage. I see people today who are out of shape, ill-tempered, flawed, and scarred. I would have a great deal of difficulty in such a marriage!

"Please do not think me proud or condescending, I assure you, that is not the case. I said what I said simply because I literally did have the perfect wife, and I myself was the perfect man! Neither of us had any physical flaws at all, and both of us walked with God.

"And that is what made a particular day in our marriage so difficult. I found myself about to lose my wife, and I found that I could not bear to live without her. That led me to do the unthinkable.

"Who am I? Why, I am the man who could have lived without her, but couldn't live without her; I am Adam."

Genesis 3:1 *Now the serpent was more subtil than any beast of the field which the LORD God had made. And* *he said unto the woman, Yea, hath God said, Ye shall not eat of every tree of the garden?* **2** *And the woman said unto the serpent, We may eat of the fruit of the trees of the garden:* **3** *But of the fruit of the tree which is in the midst of the garden, God hath said, Ye shall not eat of it, neither shall ye touch it, lest ye die.* **4** *And the serpent said unto the woman, Ye shall not surely die:* **5** *For God doth know that in the day ye eat thereof, then your eyes shall be opened, and ye shall be as gods, knowing good and evil.* **6** *And when the woman saw that the tree was good for food, and that it was pleasant to the eyes, and a tree to be desired to make one wise, she took of the fruit thereof, and did eat, and gave also unto her husband with her; and he did eat.* **7** *And the eyes of them both were opened, and they knew that they were naked; and they sewed fig leaves together, and made themselves aprons.* **8** *And they heard the voice of the LORD God walking in the garden in the cool of the day: and Adam and his wife hid themselves from the presence of the LORD God amongst the trees of the garden.* **9** *And the LORD God called unto Adam, and said unto him, Where art thou?* **10** *And he said, I heard thy voice in the garden, and I was afraid, because I was naked; and I hid myself.* **11** *And he said, Who told thee that thou wast naked? Hast thou eaten of the tree, whereof I commanded thee that thou shouldest not eat?* **12** *And the man said, The woman whom thou gavest to be with me, she gave me of the tree, and I did eat.* **13** *And the LORD God said unto the woman, What is this that thou hast done? And the woman said, The serpent beguiled me, and I did eat.* **14** *And the LORD God said unto the serpent, Because thou hast done this, thou art cursed above all cattle, and above every beast of the field; upon thy belly shalt thou go, and dust shalt thou eat all the days of thy life:* **15** *And I will put enmity between thee and the woman, and between thy seed and her seed; it shall bruise thy head, and thou shalt bruise his heel.* **16** *Unto the woman he said, I will greatly multiply thy*

124

sorrow and thy conception; in sorrow thou shalt bring forth children; and thy desire shall be to thy husband, and he shall rule over thee. **17** *And unto Adam he said, Because thou hast hearkened unto the voice of thy wife, and hast eaten of the tree, of which I commanded thee, saying, Thou shalt not eat of it: cursed is the ground for thy sake; in sorrow shalt thou eat of it all the days of thy life;* **18** *Thorns also and thistles shall it bring forth to thee; and thou shalt eat the herb of the field;* **19** *In the sweat of thy face shalt thou eat bread, till thou return unto the ground; for out of it wast thou taken: for dust thou art, and unto dust shalt thou return.* **20** *And Adam called his wife's name Eve; because she was the mother of all living.* **21** *Unto Adam also and to his wife did the LORD God make coats of skins, and clothed them.* **22** *And the LORD God said, Behold, the man is become as one of us, to know good and evil: and now, lest he put forth his hand, and take also of the tree of life, and eat, and live for ever:* **23** *Therefore the LORD God sent him forth from the garden of Eden, to till the ground from whence he was taken.* **24** *So he drove out the man; and he placed at the east of the garden of Eden Cherubims, and a flaming sword which turned every way, to keep the way of the tree of life.*

We know this account so well. It is the true to life, historical account of how mankind fell into sin. You surely know this, and you also surely know that God had very clearly warned them about this and about what would happen if they chose to disobey. In case you do not, drop back one chapter and look at it.

Genesis 2:15 *And the LORD God took the man, and put him into the garden of Eden to dress it and to keep it.* **16** *And the LORD God commanded the man, saying, Of every tree of the garden thou mayest freely eat:* **17** *But of the tree of the knowledge of good and evil, thou shalt not eat of it: for in the day that thou eatest thereof thou shalt surely die.*

Adam had been warned, and from chapter three we see that the warning had been communicated to Eve. They both knew that the tree was off limits.

When we arrive in chapter three and look at the fall of man, it is easy to assume some things that are not true. The main thing that it is easy to assume is that this was a one right after the other kind of thing. Eve ate the fruit and then Adam immediately ate the fruit, and then after they both ate the fruit, they both at the exact same time realized the terrible mistake they had made. But that is not the way it was, not at all, not by a long shot. There is a verse in the New Testament that in just a few words gives us enormous insight into how it really happened:

1 Timothy 2:13 *For Adam was first formed, then Eve.* **14** *And Adam was not deceived, but the woman being deceived was in the transgression.*

Pay attention to those words, *Adam was not deceived.* That tells us that Adam knew exactly what he was doing and what it was going to cost him. This is essential for our understanding as we apply this text to our study of marriage.

A close couple
Genesis 2:18 *And the LORD God said, It is not good that the man should be alone; I will make him an help meet for him.* **19** *And out of the ground the LORD God formed every beast of the field, and every fowl of the air; and brought them unto Adam to see what he would call them: and whatsoever Adam called every living creature, that was the name thereof.* **20** *And Adam gave names to all cattle, and to the fowl of the air, and to every beast of the field; but for Adam there was not found an help meet for him.* **21** *And the LORD God caused a deep sleep to fall upon Adam, and he slept: and he took one of his ribs, and closed up the flesh instead thereof;* **22** *And the rib, which the LORD God had*

*taken from man, made he a woman, and brought her unto
the man. 23 And Adam said, This is now bone of my bones,
and flesh of my flesh: she shall be called Woman, because
she was taken out of Man. 24 Therefore shall a man leave
his father and his mother, and shall cleave unto his wife: and
they shall be one flesh. 25 And they were both naked, the
man and his wife, and were not ashamed.*

It is very evident to anyone who slows down to
consider the text that Adam and Eve were likely the closest
married couple to ever live. They were close first of all
because of how Eve came into being. Many husbands and
wives feel like they are one flesh, but that was literally true
for Adam and Eve more than for anyone else ever. She
literally came from him! God took a part of Adam's body,
multiplied it, molded it, and made Eve from it. There was
never a moment of her entire existence that she was not part
of Adam!

They were also close because there were no sins or
flaws or mistakes to come between them. As a spouse, you
can pretty much count on being flawed and finding flaws.
You can count on making mistakes, using the wrong tone of
voice at some point, saying things a different way than you
meant them, and having your spouse do the same. You can
count on cellulite invading, eyesight fading, and your
physical condition degrading. But for Adam and Eve none
of this was an issue!

No cellulite, no bad hair days, no body odor, no bad
breath, no pot bellies, no widening hips, no cross moods, no
harsh tones of voice. These two were created utterly perfect;
they made Ken and Barbie look like Bill and Hillary!

They were also close because it was just them, no
one else. There were no jealousy issues at all between them;
Eve simply checked his ribs each night, and as long as they
were all there, everything was good!

There has never been, and will never again be, a man and wife relationship any closer than what Adam and Eve had. They were best of friends; they were the closest of lovers.

A complete condemnation

Genesis 2:17 *But of the tree of the knowledge of good and evil, thou shalt not eat of it: for in the day that thou eatest thereof thou shalt surely die.*

There was nothing ambiguous about the command that God gave them. But there was something ominous about any breaking of the command:

...for in the day that thou eatest thereof thou shalt surely die.

There is much to see here, and it is essential to our understanding that we do. We see first of all that whoever did not eat the fruit would not die, ever; they would be immortal!

We also see that the very instant anyone did eat the fruit, one death would take place and another death would begin to take place. The Bible clearly describes two types of death. One is spiritual death–separation from God.

Ephesians 2:1 *And you hath he quickened, **who were dead in trespasses and sins**; 2 Wherein in time past ye walked according to the course of this world, according to the prince of the power of the air, the spirit that now worketh in the children of disobedience: 3 Among whom also we all had our conversation in times past in the lusts of our flesh, fulfilling the desires of the flesh and of the mind; and were by nature the children of wrath, even as others. 4 But God, who is rich in mercy, for his great love wherewith he loved us, 5 Even when **we were dead in sins**, hath quickened us together with Christ, (by grace ye are saved;)*

This type of death, this separation from God, was going to take place immediately, instantaneously, in whoever ate the fruit.

The second type of death that the Bible describes is the obvious kind, physical death. This kind of death is a process, and it would begin to happen the very moment that anyone ate the fruit. Prior to that time not so much as a single cell in their body would ever die, but once someone ate the fruit, those individual cells would begin to age and die and would eventually lead to sickness, old age, and death.

Between the two deaths, there would be a complete condemnation of anyone who ever ate the fruit. God was clear on this...they both understood it...neither of them would have any excuse to disobey.

A conscious choice

Genesis 3:1 *Now the serpent was more subtil than any beast of the field which the LORD God had made. And he said unto the woman, Yea, hath God said, Ye shall not eat of every tree of the garden?* **2** *And the woman said unto the serpent, We may eat of the fruit of the trees of the garden:* **3** *But of the fruit of the tree which is in the midst of the garden, God hath said, Ye shall not eat of it, neither shall ye touch it, lest ye die.* **4** *And the serpent said unto the woman, Ye shall not surely die:* **5** *For God doth know that in the day ye eat thereof, then your eyes shall be opened, and ye shall be as gods, knowing good and evil.* **6** *And when the woman saw that the tree was good for food, and that it was pleasant to the eyes, and a tree to be desired to make one wise, she took of the fruit thereof, and did eat, and gave also unto her husband with her; and he did eat.*

Now read one more time what Paul told Timothy:

1 Timothy 2:13 *For Adam was first formed, then Eve.* **14** *And Adam was not deceived, but the woman being deceived was in the transgression.*

That truth from 1 Timothy has to be placed into the narrative of Genesis 3. If we just read Genesis 3:6 and did not have access to 1 Timothy 2:14 we may be tempted to think that what happened, happened very quickly, and that Adam really did not have time to think about it, and that he was as much caught off guard by it as Eve was. But when we put the truth of 1 Timothy 2:14 into the narrative of Genesis 3:6, we find that Adam had plenty of time to realize what Eve had done and what the consequences were. When we put the truth of 1 Timothy 2:14 into the narrative of Genesis 3:6, we find that Adam was able to clearly evaluate his choices. When we put the truth of 1 Timothy 2:14 into the narrative of Genesis 3:6, we find that Adam was able to see in Eve the beginning of the effects of sin, and realizing what those effects were, chose to follow her into that sin anyway.

Put yourself there in the garden as an observer and try to see what Adam saw.

Eve had never ever had anything but the pure innocent glow of God on her face, but the moment she took of that fruit, that innocence was gone. Her face changed just like the faces of people today who sin. That sweet innocence goes away, and people that really, really know them well can see it written on their faces.

Eve had never had any fear before, because she had always been in the familiar territory of being obedient to God and blessed by God. But the moment she took of that fruit, the natural fear of sin and consequences was written on her face. She was in unfamiliar territory, and she was in unfamiliar territory alone.

Adam knew what God had said, and he knew that God meant it. Adam knew that his wife was now dying.

Adam knew that God was now going to be angry with her.

Adam knew that he could still walk and talk with God, but Eve could not.

Adam was not some mindless dummy just because he was the first man. Having been hand created by God, having never experienced the curse of sin, and having walked and talked with God in the garden, Adam was the smartest man who ever lived. Without ever having experienced or seen it, Adam still knew what it was going to be like for Eve to grow old and die. When God told them they would die if they ate the fruit, notice that He did not have to explain it to them; Adam knew what it meant!

And Adam knew in an instant that he and Eve were now heading different directions. He knew that he would never age, but that she would.

He knew that however long it took, there would come a day when she in terror breathed her last breath and was put in the ground, but that he would still be young and healthy and immortal.

Adam knew the loneliness that Eve was already beginning to feel, and he knew that it was only going to get worse. Eve was deceived about all of this, but Adam was not. Eve believed what the devil told her, but Adam did not. As the juice from the fruit dripped down her lovely chin, Adam knew that he himself now had a choice to make.

Do I turn around and walk away? Do I leave her for God to deal with? Do I continue to stay young while she ages? Do I continue to walk and talk with God while she no longer has that option? Do I leave her to her loneliness? Do I retain my innocence and immortality while she wallows alone in her guilt and dies?

Adam had a conscious choice to make.

And he did.

Without being deceived, knowing exactly what it was going to cost, he chose aging over staying young. Without being deceived, knowing exactly what it was going to cost, he chose feeling guilt and shame over feeling nothing but innocence and purity. Without being deceived, knowing exactly what it was going to cost, he chose feeling aches and pains over never knowing a single ache or pain. Without being deceived, knowing exactly what it was going to cost, he chose to one day have his eyesight go dim. Without being deceived, knowing exactly what it was going to cost, he chose to one day have his hearing fade. Without being deceived, knowing exactly what it was going to cost, he chose to stay with his bride even if it meant dying in agony for her.

I am not for one moment justifying what Adam did. You know he sinned, I know he sinned, even he knew that he sinned. What he did was wrong. But you cannot help but admire somebody that loves his bride enough to give up so much for her!

A consequence carried

Genesis 3:17 *And unto Adam he said, Because thou hast hearkened unto the voice of thy wife, and hast eaten of the tree, of which I commanded thee, saying, Thou shalt not eat of it: cursed is the ground for thy sake; in sorrow shalt thou eat of it all the days of thy life;* **18** *Thorns also and thistles shall it bring forth to thee; and thou shalt eat the herb of the field;* **19** *In the sweat of thy face shalt thou eat bread, till thou return unto the ground; for out of it wast thou taken: for dust thou art, and unto dust shalt thou return.* **20** *And Adam called his wife's name Eve; because she was the mother of all living.* **21** *Unto Adam also and to his wife did the LORD God make coats of skins, and clothed them.* **22** *And the LORD God said, Behold, the man is become as one of us, to know good and evil: and now, lest he put forth his* *hand, and take also of the tree of life, and eat, and live for ever:* **23** *Therefore the LORD God sent him forth from the garden of Eden, to till the ground from whence he was taken.* **24** *So he drove out the man; and he placed at the east of the garden of Eden Cherubims, and a flaming sword which turned every way, to keep the way of the tree of life.*

Oh, if we could just put ourselves there on that day, if we could just see it like it was. Adam and Eve standing before God, both feeling the full weight of their guilt.

God passed the sentence on them. It is interesting to me that when He passed sentence on Eve, He actually said very little. You would expect that because she was the first one to eat the fruit that He would really come down on her, but He did not. The entire extent of what He said to her was in verse sixteen.

Genesis 3:16 *Unto the woman he said, I will greatly multiply thy sorrow and thy conception; in sorrow thou shalt bring forth children; and thy desire shall be to thy husband, and he shall rule over thee.*

Do you notice some things? Yes, she was going to die, but God did not even mention that to her. I take it that she was broken, and in His mercy, God did not bother to tell her what she already knew. She was already terrified, so God did not even mention death to her. All He mentioned was that she was going to have a lot of kids, and that it was going to hurt, and that she would have to submit to her husband. Eve had to feel like, "What? That's all He's going to say? I thought He was going to read me the riot act!"

God was going to lower the hammer. But not on Eve. The hammer of judgment would fall on Adam instead.

Genesis 3:17 *And unto Adam he said, Because thou hast hearkened unto the voice of thy wife, and hast eaten of the tree, of which I commanded thee, saying, Thou shalt not eat of it: cursed is the ground for thy sake; in sorrow shalt thou eat of it all the days of thy life;* **18** *Thorns also and*

133

*thistles shall it bring forth to thee; and thou shalt eat the herb of the field; **19** In the sweat of thy face shalt thou eat bread, till thou return unto the ground; for out of it wast thou taken: for dust thou art, and unto dust shalt thou return.*

"Adam, I am cursing the entire planet for your sake. No matter where you drop a plow, every inch of ground is going to bow up and rebel against your efforts. Adam, I am going to cause thorns and thistles to grow to scar and scratch you, and it is your fault. Adam, you had all of these fruits of the garden to eat, now I am going to make you eat herbs of the field. Adam, you are going to work, and sweat, and get tired and exhausted. Adam, you are going to grow old and die. I made you out of dust, and you disobeyed me. I am going to strip you of your immortality, your body is going to age, get sick, die, and decay all the way back to the dust you were before I made you."

God does not seem to have shown the least bit of anger toward Eve. But when it came to Adam, God just lowered the hammer, and I do not have one doubt in my mind that Adam knew that it was going to be that way.

Adam and Eve had one more thing coming, one more thing that I am completely convinced that Adam anticipated ahead of time.

Genesis 3:23 *Therefore the LORD God sent him forth from the garden of Eden, to till the ground from whence he was taken.* **24** *So he drove out the man; and he placed at the east of the garden of Eden Cherubims, and a flaming sword which turned every way, to keep the way of the tree of life.*

Adam and Eve had been able to call paradise home. Now they found themselves kicked out.

Do you understand what Adam did for the love of his bride? He gave up paradise...he gave up immortality and chose to die...he gave up being able to fellowship face to face with God...he chose to experience pain...he took Eve's sin upon himself and bore the full wrath of God for what she had done.

You and I know that there was no way Adam could fix anything spiritually, all he did was make things worse. But we also know that there was another Adam!

1 Corinthians 15:45 mentions the first Adam, but then it calls Jesus the last Adam. The old Christmas song "Hark, the Herald Angels Sing" got it right when it called Jesus the "second Adam from above."

The first Adam had a bride that came from his side...

The second Adam had a bride that came from His side too:

John 19:34 *But one of the soldiers with a spear pierced his side, and forthwith came there out blood and water.*

That soldier pierced the very heart of Jesus, and that blood and water that flowed out was just the birthing of His bride.

Revelation 21:9b... *Come hither, I will shew thee the bride, the Lamb's wife.*

The first Adam loved his bride...

The second Adam loved his bride too:

Ephesians 5:25 *Husbands, love your wives, even as Christ also loved the church, and gave himself for it;*

The first Adam saw his bride sin and fall under the condemnation of God...

The second Adam did too:

Romans 3:23 *For all have sinned, and come short of the glory of God;*

The first Adam knew that his wife was going to die for what she had done...

The second Adam did too:

Romans 6:23a *For the wages of sin is death;*

The first Adam knew that if he tried to step in and help her, he was going to have to leave paradise to do it...

135

The second Adam knew that if he tried to step in and help her, He was going to have to leave heaven to do it:

John 1:14 *And the Word was made flesh, and dwelt among us, (and we beheld his glory, the glory as of the only begotten of the Father,) full of grace and truth.*

The first Adam took his wife's sin upon himself...

The second Adam did too:

2 Corinthians 5:21 *For he hath made him to be sin for us, who knew no sin; that we might be made the righteousness of God in him.*

The first Adam stood up and willingly took the full brunt of God's wrath on himself...

The second Adam did too:

Isaiah 53:5 *But he was wounded for our transgressions, he was bruised for our iniquities: the chastisement of our peace was upon him; and with his stripes we are healed.* **6** *All we like sheep have gone astray; we have turned every one to his own way; and the LORD hath laid on him the iniquity of us all.* **7** *He was oppressed, and he was afflicted, yet he opened not his mouth: he is brought as a lamb to the slaughter, and as a sheep before her shearers is dumb, so he openeth not his mouth.* **8** *He was taken from prison and from judgment: and who shall declare his generation? for he was cut off out of the land of the living: for the transgression of my people was he stricken.*

The first Adam was cut off from God because he chose to take his wife's sin upon himself...

The second Adam was too:

Matthew 27:46 *And about the ninth hour Jesus cried with a loud voice, saying, Eli, Eli, lama sabachthani? that is to say, My God, my God, why hast thou forsaken me?*

The first Adam gave up immortality, lived a mortal life, and then breathed his last breath and died for his bride...

The second Adam did too:

John 19:30 *When Jesus therefore had received the vinegar, he said, It is finished: and he bowed his head, and gave up the ghost.*

In the spiritual sense, Jesus fixed what Adam broke!

But please pay attention: Adam and Eve were a literal man and woman with a literal marriage! And though Adam did wrong, there is something he did that can teach us a great deal about marriage.

Adam communicated to his wife that he could not possibly live without her, and that he would rather die with her than live without her.

And marriage wise, what was the result? They lived hundreds of more years together and had kids, grand kids, great-grand kids, great-great-grandkids.

Their marriage made it!

In marriage, for some reason people often communicate reservations to each other. One spouse will often get the sense from the other spouse that he or she is really not that important. Eve never got that sense from Adam!

Sir, Ma'am, examine what kind of message you are sending your spouse. In fact, do one even better than that; ask what kind of message you are sending. As for me, I want my wife to get the message from me that even though I could live without her, I cannot live without her!

137

Chapter 11
The Man Whose Marriage Had to Survive in Spite of Him

"Greetings, people of the King, and may the Lord be with you. You doubtless know me. In fact, I am known and revered, even in your day, by more than three billion people! I lived some four thousand years ago, but time has not diminished my stature among men.

"I was called the friend of God, and I was. God and I spoke often, person to person. He entrusted me with the privilege of beginning the national blood line of the Lord Jesus Christ.

"But on a more personal note, I was also a husband. My wife was utterly beautiful, even into her old age. And therein lay the problem. Not in my wife's beauty, but in my fear! I so feared that some other man may kill me for my wife that I chose to tell everyone that she was my sister.

"Naturally this made for some rather awkward moments. How does one say, 'Goodbye, Sis, enjoy your new husband!' while another man is leading his wife away? But I did so. Not once, but twice! Remarkably, our marriage somehow survived.

"Who am I? I am the man whose marriage had to survive in spite of me; I am Abraham."

Genesis 12:10 *And there was a famine in the land: and Abram went down into Egypt to sojourn there; for the famine was grievous in the land.* **11** *And it came to pass, when he was come near to enter into Egypt, that he said unto Sarai his wife, Behold now, I know that thou art a fair woman to look upon:* **12** *Therefore it shall come to pass, when the Egyptians shall see thee, that they shall say, This is his wife: and they will kill me, but they will save thee alive.* **13** *Say, I pray thee, thou art my sister: that it may be well with me for thy sake; and my soul shall live because of thee.* **14** *And it came to pass, that, when Abram was come into Egypt, the Egyptians beheld the woman that she was very fair.* **15** *The princes also of Pharaoh saw her, and commended her before Pharaoh: and the woman was taken into Pharaoh's house.* **16** *And he entreated Abram well for her sake: and he had sheep, and oxen, and he asses, and menservants, and maidservants, and she asses, and camels.* **17** *And the LORD plagued Pharaoh and his house with great plagues because of Sarai Abram's wife.* **18** *And Pharaoh called Abram, and said, What is this that thou hast done unto me? why didst thou not tell me that she was thy wife?* **19** *Why saidst thou, She is my sister? so I might have taken her to me to wife: now therefore behold thy wife, take her, and go thy way.* **20** *And Pharaoh commanded his men concerning him: and they sent him away, and his wife, and all that he had.*

Now fast forward twenty-five years:

Genesis 20:1 *And Abraham journeyed from thence toward the south country, and dwelled between Kadesh and Shur, and sojourned in Gerar.* **2** *And Abraham said of Sarah his wife, She is my sister: and Abimelech king of Gerar sent, and took Sarah.* **3** *But God came to Abimelech in a dream by night, and said to him, Behold, thou art but a dead man, for the woman which thou hast taken; for she is a man's wife.* **4** *But Abimelech had not come near her: and he said, Lord,*

140

wilt thou slay also a righteous nation? 5 Said he not unto me, She is my sister? and she, even she herself said, He is my brother: in the integrity of my heart and innocency of my hands have I done this. 6 And God said unto him in a dream, Yea, I know that thou didst this in the integrity of thy heart; for I also withheld thee from sinning against me: therefore suffered I thee not to touch her. 7 Now therefore restore the man his wife; for he is a prophet, and he shall pray for thee, and thou shalt live: and if thou restore her not, know thou that thou shalt surely die, thou, and all that are thine. 8 Therefore Abimelech rose early in the morning, and called all his servants, and told all these things in their ears: and the men were sore afraid. 9 Then Abimelech called Abraham, and said unto him, What hast thou done unto us? and what have I offended thee, that thou hast brought on me and on my kingdom a great sin? thou hast done deeds unto me that ought not to be done. 10 And Abimelech said unto Abraham, What sawest thou, that thou hast done this thing? 11 And Abraham said, Because I thought, Surely the fear of God is not in this place; and they will slay me for my wife's sake. 12 And yet indeed she is my sister; she is the daughter of my father, but not the daughter of my mother; and she became my wife. 13 And it came to pass, when God caused me to wander from my father's house, that I said unto her, This is thy kindness which thou shalt shew unto me; at every place whither we shall come, say of me, He is my brother. 14 And Abimelech took sheep, and oxen, and menservants, and womenservants, and gave them unto Abraham, and restored him Sarah his wife.

Twice, twice at the very least, and maybe a great many more times, Abraham put his own safety and security above the needs of his wife! Abraham, amazingly enough, was a marriage breaker rather than a marriage maker. His marriage survived, but it had to survive in spite of him. Let's look at it and see what we can learn.

Abraham went somewhere that was harmful to his marriage

Genesis 12:10 *And there was a famine in the land: and Abram went down into Egypt to sojourn there; for the famine was grievous in the land.* **11** *And it came to pass, when he was come near to enter into Egypt, that he said unto Sarai his wife, Behold now, I know that thou art a fair woman to look upon:* **12** *Therefore it shall come to pass, when the Egyptians shall see thee, that they shall say, This is his wife: and they will kill me, but they will save thee alive.*

Please notice something. Before Abraham ever set foot in Egypt, he knew that doing so was going to be harmful to his marriage:

...when he was come near to enter into Egypt, that he said unto Sarai his wife...

I would love to sit down with Abraham and ask him one question. Why? Why would you go somewhere that you know is going to be harmful to your marriage?

This is a far different matter from going somewhere that your wife or even your kids "do not like." Lots of wives and kids do not like going to church, or at least not to a good one. You should go anyway. But there are many places that husbands go that are harmful to their marriage. Sin establishments like bars, strip clubs, and parties. Out with friends that are bitter, hateful, or carnal. Taking a job somewhere where there is no good church or support system.

Sir, the places you go and the places you take your wife to will have a major impact on your marriage for good or for bad! Make sure, therefore, that you never take her anywhere or go anywhere that will be harmful to your marriage!

Abraham taught his family deceit

Genesis 12:13 *Say, I pray thee, thou art my sister...*

142

I would, if I had a lot of money, be willing to pay all of it to see the look on Sarah's face when he said this. Ladies, can you just imagine...

And he did it more than once!

Genesis 20:1 *And Abraham journeyed from thence toward the south country, and dwelled between Kadesh and Shur, and sojourned in Gerar. 2 And Abraham said of Sarah his wife, She is my sister: and Abimelech king of Gerar sent, and took Sarah. 3 But God came to Abimelech in a dream by night, and said to him, Behold, thou art but a dead man, for the woman which thou hast taken; for she is a man's wife. 4 But Abimelech had not come near her: and he said, Lord, wilt thou slay also a righteous nation? 5 Said he not unto me, She is my sister? and she, even she herself said, He is my brother: in the integrity of my heart and innocency of my hands have I done this.*

Abraham was a great many great things, but completely honest was not one of those things! Sarah was just his half-sister, but she was 100% his wife. Abraham was being deceitful.

And Abraham drew his wife into the deceit. I am absolutely stunned that their marriage survived.

The thing about deceit is, not only can it ruin a marriage, it can even ruin your child's marriage. The deceitful husband, or wife for that matter, may become a marriage breaker to their own children. Look ahead a great many years, please.

Genesis 26:1 *And there was a famine in the land, beside the first famine that was in the days of Abraham. And Isaac went unto Abimelech king of the Philistines unto Gerar. 2 And the LORD appeared unto him, and said, Go not down into Egypt; dwell in the land which I shall tell thee of: 3 Sojourn in this land, and I will be with thee, and will bless thee; for unto thee, and unto thy seed, I will give all these countries, and I will perform the oath which I sware*

143

unto Abraham thy father; 4 And I will make thy seed to multiply as the stars of heaven, and will give unto thy seed all these countries; and in thy seed shall all the nations of the earth be blessed; 5 Because that Abraham obeyed my voice, and kept my charge, my commandments, my statutes, and my laws. 6 And Isaac dwelt in Gerar: 7 And the men of the place asked him of his wife; and he said, She is my sister: for he feared to say, She is my wife; lest, said he, the men of the place should kill me for Rebekah; because she was fair to look upon. 8 And it came to pass, when he had been there a long time, that Abimelech king of the Philistines looked out at a window, and saw, and, behold, Isaac was sporting with Rebekah his wife. 9 And Abimelech called Isaac, and said, Behold, of a surety she is thy wife: and how saidst thou, She is my sister? And Isaac said unto him, Because I said, Lest I die for her. 10 And Abimelech said, What is this thou hast done unto us? one of the people might lightly have lien with thy wife, and thou shouldest have brought guiltiness upon us.

Abraham taught Sarah to tell a half lie, and that resulted in their son telling a whole lie! Parents, what your children see in your marriage will very likely be repeated in their marriages years down the road. Ma'am, if you have a son, you might not want to be a loud, obnoxious, wife that bosses your husband around, because one day your son is going to get married, and good luck trying to get him to be the man in his home if that is what he grew up watching. Expect him to be married to someone even more of a shrew than you.

Sir, if you have a daughter, you might not want to be an abusive jerk to your wife, because one day your daughter is going to get married, and good luck trying to get her not to be an abused doormat if that is what she grew up seeing in your home.

The same holds true for deceit. If you lie, you will probably produce children who lie. If a man as great as Abraham was not able to avoid the law of sowing and reaping on this, you are not likely to avoid it either.

But back to the issue of marriage, there is one more thing to consider on this. Sir, if you are deceitful and even go so far as to draw your wife into that deceit, may I tell you what to expect? Expect that eventually, the wife that has lied *for you* will end up lying *to you.* And that kind of thing, sir, is toxic to a marriage. Once trust is ruined, it is very difficult to ever get it back.

Twice Sarah was "taken" from him, and twice he sat back and let it happen

Genesis 12:14 *And it came to pass, that, when Abram was come into Egypt, the Egyptians beheld the woman that she was very fair.* **15** *The princes also of Pharaoh saw her, and commended her before Pharaoh: and the woman was **taken** into Pharaoh's house.*

Genesis 20:2 *And Abraham said of Sarah his wife, She is my sister: and Abimelech king of Gerar sent, and **took** Sarah.*

Can you imagine what this was like, as the knock on the door came?

I fear that scene is repeated more often than we realize in our day.

A wife is "taken" from the husband due to all of the big boy toys that have been purchased on credit, necessitating that the wife go to work full time.

Does a wife often have to work for "needs?" Certainly, and there is nothing wrong with that. But I am telling you, you better be very careful not to go into debt for toys, or you will find that those toys have "taken" your wife from you to help pay for them!

A wife is "taken" from the husband because of continuous extra-curricular activities for the kids.

I spoke to a lost man sometime back, and even he was able to understand this. He told me, "Our kids were in one thing after another: soccer, cheering, basketball, dance, on and on. It was so bad that every night of the week we were going different directions taking them to all of it. Finally I said, 'This has to stop, or we aren't going to have a marriage.' And so we stopped it. They can do one activity at a time, and they have to take turns, so that we can do what we do together, as a family, and so that we can actually have time at home together."

Smart man!

Sir, ma'am, may I remind you of something obvious that the world now regards as heresy? Your children are not to be the most important people in your life; your spouse is to be the most important person in your life:

Genesis 2:24 *Therefore shall a man leave his father and his mother, and shall cleave unto his wife: and they shall be* ***one flesh***.

Matthew 19:6 *Wherefore they are no more twain, but* ***one flesh***. *What therefore God hath joined together, let not man put asunder.*

I have known quite a lot of people who allowed their children to destroy their marriage! Sir, do not ever let your wife be "taken" from you by unending extracurricular activities for your children. If it does not destroy your marriage while they are at home, it will likely do so once they are gone, because you two will not even know each other, since your world has revolved around your kids for so long.

And may I say a word right here to preachers? Sir, you better be careful not to let the ministry "take" your wife. I am blown away by something that God had to say to Abimilech in Genesis 20:7:

Genesis 20:7 *Now therefore restore the man his wife; for he is a prophet...*

May I paraphrase that? God said, "Hey! Give the preacher his wife back."

Preacher, the very first thing that your wife is, is your wife. That comes first. It comes before her being a Sunday school teacher or pianist or bus worker or cleaner or secretary or nursery worker or anything else ministry related. Make sure you do not load her down with so many ministerial responsibilities that your wife is "taken" from you by the ministry!

Abraham did not grow in his marriage through the years, he stayed the same husband he had always been... which was not a good thing

There are twenty-five years between chapters twelve and twenty. Abraham had a very bad experience in chapter twelve and twenty-five years to learn from it, yet he did the exact same thing again!

Husbands, you ought not just to grow in your "girth" through the years, you should also grow in your "worth" through the years! You should become more godly and more kind and more loving and more wise every single year of your marriage.

It will not happen by accident.

Ask your wife for tips on improvement.

Study your Bible as to how you should behave as a husband.

Read good Bible based books on the subject.

Above all, learn from your mistakes and never ever repeat them!

Abraham put his well-being before that of his wife

Genesis 12:13 *Say, I pray thee, thou art my sister: that it may be well with me for thy sake; and my soul shall live because of thee.*

Abraham and Sarah had such a...*unique* relationship. Do you remember what she said to him in the Hagar situation, where she convinced him to sleep with their maid, and Hagar got pregnant by him?

Genesis 16:5 *And Sarai said unto Abram, **My wrong be upon thee**: I have given my maid into thy bosom; and when she saw that she had conceived, I was despised in her eyes: the LORD judge between me and thee.*

My wrong be upon thee! That is hilarious! But where did she learn that kind of nonsense from? From her husband, who said, "*Say, I pray thee, thou art my sister: **that it may be well with me** for thy sake*"

"Hey, honey, tell you what. Tell those dudes that you're my sister, so that everything will go good for me, and you know, so I won't have any trouble or anything!"

Once again, can you even imagine?

Abraham, marriage breaker Abraham, was putting his well-being ahead of that of his wife. Men, this is an excellent way to destroy your marriage. Here is a better option:

Philippians 2:2 *Fulfil ye my joy, that ye be likeminded, having the same love, being of one accord, of one mind.* **3** *Let nothing be done through strife or vainglory; but in lowliness of mind let each esteem other better than themselves.*

Now that will make a marriage! Putting your wife ahead of yourself will build your marriage.

148

Abraham did not put the same effort into his marriage as he did into everything else

Think of his rescue of Lot. In Genesis 14, Lot was taken captive by enemy armies. Abraham, though, had spent many years training and supplying 318 servants in his own household to fight. He took those trained men, pursued the enemies, beat them, and brought Lot back home. That took an amazing amount of effort for a sniveling little nephew!

Think of his willingness to let Lot choose the best of the land, while he himself took the leftovers in Genesis 13.

Think of his intercession for Sodom and Gomorrah in Genesis 18.

Abraham was a man who put maximum effort into everything that he ever did. Everything, that is, except his marriage!

Sir, if you found out that you had cancer, how hard would you fight it to try and live?

Put that same kind of effort into your marriage.

I have done marriage counseling for over twenty years as of the writing of this book. It is often rewarding, but it is often frustrating enough to make me nearly pull my hair out. I will never forget counseling with a woman and her husband, and this guy was just a little weasel. How much of a weasel? He secretly brought a recorder with him into a counseling session to try to goad me into saying something wrong, so that he would have an excuse not to come to counseling anymore, and proof that I was not a good counselor! This is the kind of garbage preachers have to deal with, so pray for them!

During the counseling sessions, the wife really tried, but Mr. I. M. Weasely did not try at all. Not even a little. Finally I said, "Sir, you made a vow that went like this, 'For better or for worse, till death do us part.' Keep your vow." To which Mr. I. M. Weasely responded, "Then I'm already dead. I'm emotionally dead..."

149

No, you're a woman in disguise, that's what you are. Take your Midol and calm your hormones down.

I am forever amazed at how a man will have a decent wife, yet put no effort into the marriage. Sir, other than your walk with Christ, there is not one thing on earth that you should put greater effort into than your marriage.

In the book Letters to Phillip marriage counselor Charles Shedd tells of a man that was not putting great effort into his marriage, and because of that, the marriage was dying. He said that the man called him out to go duck hunting with him, mostly so that they could talk about marriage. Shedd got his old gun, went over to the guy's house, crawled into the boat with him, and they went out a ways into the water and talked softly while they hunted.

Shedd's gun was old and very beat up. By contrast, the husband's guns were all immaculate. Shedd noted that when the man pulled a gun out of the case, it smelled like banana oil, because the man always kept his guns oiled up. There was not a scratch on any of them.

At one point, Shedd laid his gun down in the bottom of the boat. The man went ballistic. He chewed him out for not taking care of his gun. Shedd said, "You know, if he had put nearly as much effort into taking care of his marriage as he did into taking care of his guns, his marriage would be just fine..."

Boys, one day (hopefully) all of you will be married. And if you are like most guys, you are going to put all of your effort into *getting married* and then little to no effort at all into *staying married*. Tend to your marriage, make it the thing that you put more effort into than anything else other than your walk with Christ.

Abraham and Sarah stayed married till death did them part. But do you know what they had to endure along the way? Two separations, one "other woman," at least one massive argument, and a whole lot of needless hard times.

Men, it does not have to be that way. Make sure that your marriage does not have to survive in spite of you.

Chapter 12
The Man Who Destroyed His Marriage by Living Like a Philistine

"Greetings, people who are far inferior to myself. It is doubtless a great joy to you to receive correspondence from someone so famous as I.

"I am usually known by the company I kept with a certain woman of ill repute. What is less commonly known is that I was once a married man!

"Sadly, the marriage did not last long. In fact, it never really even got started well before it was over!

"Had my wife and I been different from each other, things perhaps would have turned out better in our marriage. Does that sound surprising? It should not, not when one of us was a Philistine! Those wretched creatures were known for their sin, their lack of self-control, and their poor moral character. In short, they, including my wife, were just like me, and I was just like them.

"But I was not a Philistine. I was an Israelite, and a very special one. I was raised up by God to be a deliverer to my people. But instead, I chose to live my life on the lowest level possible. That destroyed a great many things, but the very first thing it destroyed was my marriage.

"Who am I? I am the man who destroyed my marriage by living like a Philistine; I am Samson."

Judges 14:1 *And Samson went down to Timnath, and saw a woman in Timnath of the daughters of the Philistines. 2 And he came up, and told his father and his mother, and said, I have seen a woman in Timnath of the daughters of the Philistines: now therefore get her for me to wife. 3 Then his father and his mother said unto him, Is there never a woman among the daughters of thy brethren, or among all my people, that thou goest to take a wife of the uncircumcised Philistines? And Samson said unto his father, Get her for me; for she pleaseth me well. 4 But his father and his mother knew not that it was of the LORD, that he sought an occasion against the Philistines: for at that time the Philistines had dominion over Israel. 5 Then went Samson down, and his father and his mother, to Timnath, and came to the vineyards of Timnath: and, behold, a young lion roared against him. 6 And the Spirit of the LORD came mightily upon him, and he rent him as he would have rent a kid, and he had nothing in his hand: but he told not his father or his mother what he had done. 7 And he went down, and talked with the woman; and she pleased Samson well. 8 And after a time he returned to take her, and he turned aside to see the carcase of the lion: and, behold, there was a swarm of bees and honey in the carcase of the lion. 9 And he took thereof in his hands, and went on eating, and came to his father and mother, and he gave them, and they did eat: but he told not them that he had taken the honey out of the carcase of the lion. 10 So his father went down unto the woman: and Samson made there a feast; for so used the young men to do. 11 And it came to pass, when they saw him, that they brought thirty companions to be with him. 12 And Samson said unto them, I will now put forth a riddle unto you: if ye can certainly declare it me within the seven days of the feast, and find it* *out, then I will give you thirty sheets and thirty change of garments:* **13** *But if ye cannot declare it me, then shall ye give me thirty sheets and thirty change of garments. And they said unto him, Put forth thy riddle, that we may hear it.* **14** *And he said unto them, Out of the eater came forth meat, and out of the strong came forth sweetness. And they could not in three days expound the riddle.* **15** *And it came to pass on the seventh day, that they said unto Samson's wife, Entice thy husband, that he may declare unto us the riddle, lest we burn thee and thy father's house with fire: have ye called us to take that we have? is it not so?* **16** *And Samson's wife wept before him, and said, Thou dost but hate me, and lovest me not: thou hast put forth a riddle unto the children of my people, and hast not told it me. And he said unto her, Behold, I have not told it my father nor my mother, and shall I tell it thee?* **17** *And she wept before him the seven days, while their feast lasted: and it came to pass on the seventh day, that he told her, because she lay sore upon him: and she told the riddle to the children of her people.* **18** *And the men of the city said unto him on the seventh day before the sun went down, What is sweeter than honey? and what is stronger than a lion? And he said unto them, If ye had not plowed with my heifer, ye had not found out my riddle.* **19** *And the Spirit of the LORD came upon him, and he went down to Ashkelon, and slew thirty men of them, and took their spoil, and gave change of garments unto them which expounded the riddle. And his anger was kindled, and he went up to his father's house.* **20** *But Samson's wife was given to his companion, whom he had used as his friend.*

Judges 15:1 *But it came to pass within a while after, in the time of wheat harvest, that Samson visited his wife with a kid; and he said, I will go in to my wife into the chamber. But her father would not suffer him to go in.* **2** *And her father said, I verily thought that thou hadst utterly hated her; therefore I gave her to thy companion: is not her*

155

younger sister fairer than she? take her, I pray thee, instead of her. **3** *And Samson said concerning them, Now shall I be more blameless than the Philistines, though I do them a displeasure.* **4** *And Samson went and caught three hundred foxes, and took firebrands, and turned tail to tail, and put a firebrand in the midst between two tails.* **5** *And when he had set the brands on fire, he let them go into the standing corn of the Philistines, and burnt up both the shocks, and also the standing corn, with the vineyards and olives.* **6** *Then the Philistines said, Who hath done this? And they answered, Samson, the son in law of the Timnite, because he had taken his wife, and given her to his companion. And the Philistines came up, and burnt her and her father with fire.*

In the life of Samson, the woman that he is automatically known for is Delilah, but Delilah was not the only woman in the life of Samson. In fact, Samson was an absolute fornicating womanizer.

In Judges 16:1, we find Samson sleeping with a prostitute.

In Judges 14:3 we find Samson's parents saying *"Is there **never** a woman among the daughters of thy brethren, or among all my people, that thou goest to take a wife of the uncircumcised Philistines?"* This lets us know that there had been woman after woman already in the life of Samson, before his wife, before the prostitute, and before Delilah.

All of these women had one thing in common, all of them were Philistines. Believe me, that is very significant.

The Philistines were the bitter enemies of everything about God and about His people. They were sexually impure, they were hateful, they were immoral. They had defeated and subjugated the people of God, the Israelites, and Samson had been raised up by God to defeat them and set His people free.

But Samson had a problem. The only time he could ever seem to regard the Philistines as enemies was when they

156

did something to him. It never mattered to him what they had done and were doing to his people, as long as they were not doing anything to him, he was their best buddy.

And then Samson got married. He got married to a Philistine girl. If Samson had somehow decided to behave like a child of God, maybe the marriage would have stood at least a slim chance. It would have been very slim, since he had already married a heathen. But Samson took slim odds of success and turned them into zero chance for success when he lived as a husband just as much like a heathen as his wife was!

In our marriages, any unbiblical behavior ought to be regarded as "Philistine behavior" and avoided.

Let's work our way through this and study the mistakes of Samson the husband.

Samson verbally placed his parents above his wife
Judges 14:7 *And he went down, and talked with the woman; and she pleased Samson well.* **8** *And after a time he returned to take her, and he turned aside to see the carcase of the lion: and, behold, there was a swarm of bees and honey in the carcase of the lion.* **9** *And he took thereof in his hands, and went on eating, and came to his father and mother, and he gave them, and they did eat: but he told not them that he had taken the honey out of the carcase of the lion.* **10** *So his father went down unto the woman: and Samson made there a feast; for so used the young men to do.* **11** *And it came to pass, when they saw him, that they brought thirty companions to be with him.* **12** *And Samson said unto them, I will now put forth a riddle unto you: if ye can certainly declare it me within the seven days of the feast, and find it out, then I will give you thirty sheets and thirty change of garments:* **13** *But if ye cannot declare it me, then shall ye give me thirty sheets and thirty change of garments. And they said unto him, Put forth thy riddle, that we may hear it.* **14**

And he said unto them, Out of the eater came forth meat, and out of the strong came forth sweetness. And they could not in three days expound the riddle. 15 And it came to pass on the seventh day, that they said unto Samson's wife, Entice thy husband, that he may declare unto us the riddle, lest we burn thee and thy father's house with fire: have ye called us to take that we have? is it not so? 16 And Samson's wife wept before him, and said, Thou dost but hate me, and lovest me not: thou hast put forth a riddle unto the children of my people, and hast not told it me. And he said unto her, Behold, I have not told it my father nor my mother, and shall I tell it thee?

By the time of Judges 14, Samson was already well on the way to destroying his usefulness for God. In fact, he broke two out of the three parts of the vow of the Nazarite all within just a couple of verses.

In verse five we find him in a vineyard, when he was never to have anything to do with the fruit of the vine.

In verse nine, Samson saw the honey in the carcass of the lion. He liked honey. He wanted honey. But a Nazarite was forbidden from touching any dead body.

That did not matter to Samson. He liked honey. He wanted honey. So he reached down into that dead carcass and took the honey.

One verse later we find Samson making a feast for his Philistine buddies; the heathen nations were in the habit of drinking at their feasts.

But not only was Samson very early on destroying his ministry, he was also very early on destroying his marriage. While Samson was in the vineyard, he met up with a wild lion. The lion decided to eat Samson, and Samson decided not to let him. When the battle was over, barehanded Samson had killed the lion.

Later, Samson came back through that way, saw the dead lion, saw the honey, and took the honey. Then, when he got to the wedding feast, he saw an opportunity to make a profit. He decided to gamble with his Philistine buddies. His game of chance was a riddle guessing game. So he made a bet with them, they agreed to the terms, and he then put forth his riddle:

"Out of the eater came forth meat, and out of the strong came forth sweetness."

That is it; that is the riddle. Yes, I know, it sounds pretty ridiculous to our western minds. But it is exactly what eastern minds were used to. Despite that, these guys were really stumped. So, seeing their money drifting away, they decided to look for an inside advantage. And they found it in Samson's wife. They threatened her life and the life of her parents if she did not tell them the riddle.

Now, the funny thing is, she had already been trying to get him to tell her! It was a seven day long feast, they came to her on the third day, but verse seventeen says that she had been pressing him about it all seven days!

And here is where Samson made his first mistake with his new wife.

Judges 14:16 *And Samson's wife wept before him, and said, Thou dost but hate me, and lovest me not: thou hast put forth a riddle unto the children of my people, and hast not told it me. And he said unto her,* ***Behold, I have not told it my father nor my mother, and shall I tell it thee?***

Do you understand what Samson was saying? He just told his wife, "I haven't even told my mom and dad the riddle; why would I tell you?" In other words, Samson verbally placed his parents above his wife.

Men, it is possible that your wife will one day be wrong about something and your parents be right about it. If that happens, you should be man enough to lovingly tell your wife that she is wrong. But there should never, ever, ever, ever, ever, ever be a time where you speak words that place your parents in a position of importance above your wife.

159

Lulu and Bubba have a date night planned. But at the last minute Bubba's mommer calls and says, "Bubber, I need you to cum sit with me fer a while; we ain't had no mommer/son time fer at least a week!"

And Bubba says, "Sorry, Lulu, mommer needs me; we'll go to the frog giggin contest next year..."

Cletus and Lurlene are sitting down to dinner, a fine possum stew that Lurlene has slaved over all day. Cletus looks at it and says, "Mommer makes it differnt thayun this; I like mommer's way better..."

Sally June is about to have to whop little Junior on the hind end, because little Junior is behaving like a brat. Then her mommer-in-law says, "You leave that yungun alone; don't you be whoppin him on the hind end!"

And Sally June's husband, Larry June, takes mommer's side, and says, "Yeah, listen to mommer; don't you be whoppin that yungun!"

Men, let me repeat myself. It is possible that your wife will one day be wrong about something and your parents be right about it. If that happens, you should be man enough to lovingly tell your wife that she is wrong. But there should never, ever, ever, ever, ever, ever be a time where you speak words that place your parents in a position of importance above your wife.

He spoke of her in derogatory terms

Judges 14:17 *And she wept before him the seven days, while their feast lasted: and it came to pass on the seventh day, that he told her, because she lay sore upon him: and she told the riddle to the children of her people.* **18** *And the men of the city said unto him on the seventh day before the sun went down, What is sweeter than honey? and what is stronger than a lion? And he said unto them, If ye had not plowed with my **heifer**, ye had not found out my riddle.*

160

Samson was clearly upset when he realized what had happened. And so, he chose to call his wife a heifer. Listen to me carefully; that was highly derogatory. Is it any wonder that their marriage did not survive? Sir, I do not care what happens in your home, you are never to speak of or to your wife in derogatory terms.

"But preacher, preacher, what about when we fight? Surely I can call her a heifer then, right?"

May I show you from the Bible a good way to fight?

Song of Solomon 5:2 *I sleep, but my heart waketh: it is the voice of my beloved that knocketh, saying, Open to me, my sister, my love, my dove, my undefiled: for my head is filled with dew, and my locks with the drops of the night.* **3** *I have put off my coat; how shall I put it on? I have washed my feet; how shall I defile them?* **4** *My beloved put in his hand by the hole of the door, and my bowels were moved for him.* **5** *I rose up to open to my beloved; and my hands dropped with myrrh, and my fingers with sweet smelling myrrh, upon the handles of the lock.* **6** *I opened to my beloved; but my beloved had withdrawn himself, and was gone: my soul failed when he spake: I sought him, but I could not find him; I called him, but he gave me no answer.*

In this passage, there is a doozy of a marital spat taking place. It was serious enough that he ended up gone for the night, and she had to chase after him! But did you notice what terms were used during this fight? Look at it again:

Song of Solomon 5:2 *I sleep, but my heart waketh: it is the voice of my **beloved** that knocketh, saying, Open to me, my sister, my love, my dove, my undefiled: for my head is filled with dew, and my locks with the drops of the night.* **3** *I have put off my coat; how shall I put it on? I have washed my feet; how shall I defile them?* **4** *My **beloved** put in his hand by the hole of the door, and my bowels were moved for him.* **5** *I rose up to open to my **beloved**; and my hands*

161

dropped with myrrh, and my fingers with sweet smelling myrrh, upon the handles of the lock. **6** *I opened to my* **beloved***; but my* **beloved** *had withdrawn himself, and was gone: my soul failed when he spake: I sought him, but I could not find him; I called him, but he gave me no answer.*

Beloved, beloved, beloved. This is how they fought. No wonder this fight ended up the way we see it end up:

Song of Solomon 6:4 *Thou art beautiful, O my love...*

During their fight she used "beloved, beloved, beloved," and at the end of the fight he was saying to her "Thou art beautiful, O my love..."

Sir, and ma'am as well, when you fight, use tender terms, not hurtful terms. If you do, there will be no damage when the fight is over. But if you call each other unkind names, the memory of those hurtful words will last years longer than the argument itself.

When the marriage got tough, Samson let his emotions take over

Judges 14:19 *And the Spirit of the LORD came upon him, and he went down to Ashkelon, and slew thirty men of them, and took their spoil, and gave change of garments unto them which expounded the riddle. And his anger was kindled,* **and he went up to his father's house***.*

It is incumbent upon everyone, man or wife, to be steady in the marriage. But it is especially important for the husband to be very steady, and when trouble comes to be very sure not to be driven by emotions. Sir, there ought not to be any bailing out in you. There ought not to be any unchecked emotion in you. You ought to never run home to mama and daddy. Marry right and then act right within the marriage.

Samson was the "believer" in the marriage! Samson was the one who should have been setting the example. But Samson got *angry*...

Sir, you are not allowed to be emotionally driven. God made you a creature of reason, not a creature of reaction. And if the devil ever finds out that you are emotionally driven, believe me, he will exploit it.

Proverbs 25:28 *He that hath no rule over his own spirit is like a city that is broken down, and without walls.*

This paints a picture of a person who is emotionally driven as being utterly defenseless! If the devil finds out that trouble will get you torn out of the frame and behaving emotionally, he will push your buttons! Settle down, sir.

Samson let his emotions run wild, and as a result, he stormed back home to mama and daddy for a while.

And here is what happened while he was gone:

Judges 14:20 *But Samson's wife was given to his companion, whom he had used as his friend.*

That never, ever would have happened if he had been there!

Samson did wrong, but instead of actually making things right, he just decided to pick back up in the bedroom

Judges 15:1 *But it came to pass within a while after, in the time of wheat harvest, that Samson visited his wife with a kid; and he said, I will go in to my wife into the chamber. But her father would not suffer him to go in.*

In Judges 15:1, we find something that married people will understand very well. It is difficult for a man to stay angry forever, because he gets "frisky feeling" after a while.

That happened to Samson. He had a knock down drag out fight with his wife, stormed off in anger, stayed gone for days and maybe weeks or months, but eventually he decided to come back. And when he did, he had one

163

particular room of the house in mind. Samson was not coming back for the kitchen, or the dining room, or the library, he was coming back for the bedroom, the "chamber."

But listen to me very well, Samson had not even begun to make things right! He had gotten out of God's will by breaking his vows, he had gambled, he had insulted his wife, he had blown a gasket and stormed back to mama and daddy's house. He had done great, great wrong!

But he never did apologize.

He never did face his wrongs.

He just decided to "let bygones be bygones" and jump right back into bed.

Sir, that is not going to work so well...

Do you know what a real man does when he has hurt his wife? He apologizes, without making any excuses:

Proverbs 28:13 *He that covereth his sins shall not prosper: but whoso confesseth and forsaketh them shall have mercy.*

Have you ever heard of "sweeping things under the rug?" That is what this verse describes, and it is especially dangerous in the home. Sir, if you have hurt your wife, get it out in the open, deal with, apologize for it, and set things right.

Samson treated his wife badly in the eyes and ears of others

When Samson came back, he found out that his wife was not his wife anymore. She had been given to someone else. And why did her father do this? He tells us in verse two.

Judges 15:2 *And her father said, **I verily thought that thou hadst utterly hated her**; therefore I gave her to thy companion: is not her younger sister fairer than she? take her, I pray thee, instead of her.*

164

Why did her father think that Samson hated her? When he called her a heifer, he did so publically. When he stormed out on the marriage, he did so publically.

Men need to learn something. That which is kept private is much easier to deal with than that which is made public. When you run your wife down to others, you will make it very nearly impossible to ever set things completely right. When you run your wife down to others, you draw them into the situation, and they end up lining up against you because of how you are treating her.

People do not like to see a woman mistreated, and they will recommend that she move on with her life without you if they see it happening. Is that right? Right is not the issue for you, sir, reality is the issue at that point. When you mistreat your wife publically, you are a fool if you think people are going to be clamoring for the two of you to get back together.

The behavior of Samson was positively heathen. He acted more like a Philistine than the Philistines did. Sir, that is a great way to become a marriage breaker.

Chapter 13
When Marriage Maker Meets Marriage Breaker

"Greetings, people whom my wife would speak kindly of, but whom I regard as inferiors. It is our understanding that you are engaged in a study of marriage. Perhaps our story can be of some assistance to you.

"My wife was an idealist. She was the kind of woman who would read her Bible, feed the homeless, and give clothing to rabble out in the cold. In short, she was silly.

"I myself, though, was a firm, practical man. I read, as long as it is a business journal. The homeless are not my problem. The rabble out in the cold can simply stay there, and stay cold. I do not care; they are not my problem either.

"Am I miserable? No! I am perfectly happy. Give me my wine, give me my money, and I will throw a feast fit for a king...a feast in celebration of myself! Why should I care for others? I am far too wise for that.

"Not that people were smart enough to understand that, mind you. Even my parents misunderstood my greatness. They named me 'fool.' Imagine that! Well, I showed them. And I showed my wife. I showed them all how great I was!

"My wife was lucky to have someone like me, though I doubt if she ever understood that.

"Who are we? Why, we are the marriage breaker married to the marriage maker, we are Nabal and Abigail."

1 Samuel 25:1 *And Samuel died; and all the Israelites were gathered together, and lamented him, and buried him in his house at Ramah. And David arose, and went down to the wilderness of Paran.* **2** *And there was a man in Maon, whose possessions were in Carmel; and the man was very great, and he had three thousand sheep, and a thousand goats: and he was shearing his sheep in Carmel.* **3** *Now the name of the man was Nabal; and the name of his wife Abigail: and she was a woman of good understanding, and of a beautiful countenance: but the man was churlish and evil in his doings; and he was of the house of Caleb.* **4** *And David heard in the wilderness that Nabal did shear his sheep.* **5** *And David sent out ten young men, and David said unto the young men, Get you up to Carmel, and go to Nabal, and greet him in my name:* **6** *And thus shall ye say to him that liveth in prosperity, Peace be both to thee, and peace be to thine house, and peace be unto all that thou hast.* **7** *And now I have heard that thou hast shearers: now thy shepherds which were with us, we hurt them not, neither was there ought missing unto them, all the while they were in Carmel.* **8** *Ask thy young men, and they will shew thee. Wherefore let the young men find favour in thine eyes: for we come in a good day: give, I pray thee, whatsoever cometh to thine hand unto thy servants, and to thy son David.* **9** *And when David's young men came, they spake to Nabal according to all those words in the name of David, and ceased.* **10** *And Nabal answered David's servants, and said, Who is David? and who is the son of Jesse? there be many servants now a days that break away every man from his master.* **11** *Shall I then take my bread, and my water, and my flesh that I have killed* *for my shearers, and give it unto men, whom I know not whence they be?* **12** *So David's young men turned their way, and went again, and came and told him all those sayings.* **13** *And David said unto his men, Gird ye on every man his sword. And they girded on every man his sword; and David also girded on his sword: and there went up after David about four hundred men; and two hundred abode by the stuff.* **14** *But one of the young men told Abigail, Nabal's wife, saying, Behold, David sent messengers out of the wilderness to salute our master; and he railed on them.* **15** *But the men were very good unto us, and we were not hurt, neither missed we any thing, as long as we were conversant with them, when we were in the fields:* **16** *They were a wall unto us both by night and day, all the while we were with them keeping the sheep.* **17** *Now therefore know and consider what thou wilt do; for evil is determined against our master, and against all his household: for he is such a son of Belial, that a man cannot speak to him.* **18** *Then Abigail made haste, and took two hundred loaves, and two bottles of wine, and five sheep ready dressed, and five measures of parched corn, and an hundred clusters of raisins, and two hundred cakes of figs, and laid them on asses.* **19** *And she said unto her servants, Go on before me; behold, I come after you. But she told not her husband Nabal.* **20** *And it was so, as she rode on the ass, that she came down by the covert of the hill, and, behold, David and his men came down against her; and she met them.* **21** *Now David had said, Surely in vain have I kept all that this fellow hath in the wilderness, so that nothing was missed of all that pertained unto him: and he hath requited me evil for good.* **22** *So and more also do God unto the enemies of David, if I leave of all that pertain to him by the morning light any that pisseth against the wall.* **23** *And when Abigail saw David, she hasted, and lighted off the ass, and fell before David on her face, and bowed herself to the ground,* **24** *And fell at his feet, and said, Upon me, my lord,* *upon me let this iniquity be: and let thine handmaid, I pray thee, speak in thine audience, and hear the words of thine handmaid.* **25** *Let not my lord, I pray thee, regard this man of Belial, even Nabal: for as his name is, so is he; Nabal is his name, and folly is with him: but I thine handmaid saw not the young men of my lord, whom thou didst send.* **26** *Now therefore, my lord, as the LORD liveth, and as thy soul liveth, seeing the LORD hath withholden thee from coming to shed blood, and from avenging thyself with thine own hand, now let thine enemies, and they that seek evil to my lord, be as Nabal.* **27** *And now this blessing which thine handmaid hath brought unto my lord, let it even be given unto the young men that follow my lord.* **28** *I pray thee, forgive the trespass of thine handmaid: for the LORD will certainly make my lord a sure house; because my lord fighteth the battles of the LORD, and evil hath not been found in thee all thy days.* **29** *Yet a man is risen to pursue thee, and to seek thy soul: but the soul of my lord shall be bound in the bundle of life with the LORD thy God; and the souls of thine enemies, them shall he sling out, as out of the middle of a sling.* **30** *And it shall come to pass, when the LORD shall have done to my lord according to all the good that he hath spoken concerning thee, and shall have appointed thee ruler over Israel;* **31** *That this shall be no grief unto thee, nor offence of heart unto my lord, either that thou hast shed blood causeless, or that my lord hath avenged himself: but when the LORD shall have dealt well with my lord, then remember thine handmaid.* **32** *And David said to Abigail, Blessed be the LORD God of Israel, which sent thee this day to meet me:* **33** *And blessed be thy advice, and blessed be thou, which hast kept me this day from coming to shed blood, and from avenging myself with mine own hand.* **34** *For in very deed, as the LORD God of Israel liveth, which hath kept me back from hurting thee, except thou hadst hasted and come to meet me, surely there had not been left* *unto Nabal by the morning light any that pisseth against the wall.* **35** *So David received of her hand that which she had brought him, and said unto her, Go up in peace to thine house; see, I have hearkened to thy voice, and have accepted thy person.* **36** *And Abigail came to Nabal; and, behold, he held a feast in his house, like the feast of a king; and Nabal's heart was merry within him, for he was very drunken: wherefore she told him nothing, less or more, until the morning light.* **37** *But it came to pass in the morning, when the wine was gone out of Nabal, and his wife had told him these things, that his heart died within him, and he became as a stone.* **38** *And it came to pass about ten days after, that the LORD smote Nabal, that he died.* **39** *And when David heard that Nabal was dead, he said, Blessed be the LORD, that hath pleaded the cause of my reproach from the hand of Nabal, and hath kept his servant from evil: for the LORD hath returned the wickedness of Nabal upon his own head. And David sent and communed with Abigail, to take her to him to wife.* **40** *And when the servants of David were come to Abigail to Carmel, they spake unto her, saying, David sent us unto thee, to take thee to him to wife.* **41** *And she arose, and bowed herself on her face to the earth, and said, Behold, let thine handmaid be a servant to wash the feet of the servants of my lord.* **42** *And Abigail hasted, and arose, and rode upon an ass, with five damsels of hers that went after her; and she went after the messengers of David, and became his wife.*

We have in our text the amazing account of Nabal and Abigail. These two had to be the most mismatched couple in the entire Bible. Look at how God Himself describes them:

1 Samuel 25:3 *Now the name of the man was Nabal; and the name of his wife Abigail: and* **she was a woman of good understanding, and of a beautiful countenance:** *but*

171

the man was churlish [cruel, difficult, stubborn] ***and evil in his doings****; and he was of the house of Caleb.*

That, friends, is night and day. Bear in mind that in those days, the women often did not get much of a choice in who they married. I have to believe that, as smart as Abigail was, this had to have been one of those occasions. It surely had to be her parents or some other guardian that married her off to this guy. I just do not believe she ever would have voluntarily married a person like Nabal!

Nonetheless, they ended up married. She was a marriage maker; he was a marriage breaker. And do you know the really ironic thing? They both ended up succeeding! How is that possible? She managed to stay married to him "till death did them part," so she succeeded in making the marriage. But he managed to behave in such a way that he died well before his time, so he succeeded in breaking the marriage! Let's study their marriage and see what we can learn. The first three will deal with things that need to be considered well before a marriage ever takes place.

While it is important for a man to do well in regards to finances, just the simple fact that a man does well in regards to finances does not automatically make him a good choice for a mate
1 Samuel 25:1 *And Samuel died; and all the Israelites were gathered together, and lamented him, and buried him in his house at Ramah. And David arose, and went down to the wilderness of Paran. 2 And there was a man in Maon, whose possessions were in Carmel; and the man was very great, and he had three thousand sheep, and a thousand goats: and he was shearing his sheep in Carmel.*

As the story begins, we find turmoil in Israel. David was on the run from Saul, trying desperately to avoid being killed. Samuel the prophet and priest had gotten old, and finally he died. Israel mourned their beloved prophet, but David had double sorrow since he was afraid that he would soon be joining Samuel in death at the hand of Saul.

In the midst of all of the national and personal mourning, there was one man who was not mourning. In fact, he was having himself quite a time. His name was Nabal, and he was rich. Verse two describes him as "great," meaning that, when we use the word "rich," we mean REALLY rich. Three thousand sheep and a thousand goats was Rockefeller type of money in those days.

Nabal was very, very good with money. Nabal did not need any help from a financial advisor. He did not bother to listen to any Dave Ramsey types giving lectures; Nabal already had the money thing figured out.

Having skill with finances is, in my judgment, a prerequisite of getting married. With my daughters, I can tell you that on any prospective suitors for them I am going to be doing a background check, a credit check, an academic records check, and a cooties check. No one who fails any of those checks needs apply. Especially the credit check! If a young man does not know how to pay all of his bills, stay out of debt, hold down a job, and invest for the future, then he needs to go somewhere safe to look for a wife. Like, China, for instance.

Nabal, for all of his flaws, had this one thing going for him that would seem to make him an attractive mate for a girl. But the thing is, while it is important for a man to do well in regards to finances, just the simple fact that a man does well in regards to finances does not automatically make him a good choice for a mate!

Parents and single young people, listen to me very carefully. The citizen in the far country did well with his finances. High end prostitutes do well with their finances. Hugh Heffner does well with his finances. Miley Cyrus does

173

well with her finances. But do you really think that any of them would make an acceptable mate?

Money is important, but it surely is not THAT important. There may come a day when you need to look past someone who is rich in order to find someone who will actually be a good spouse!

There was a girl I knew years ago before I ever met Dana. She met a guy who really knew how to make the money, I mean he brought it in hand over fist. But he was a jerk, too. Nonetheless, she married him. I was sitting at a stop light one day, and she pulled up beside me. She motioned for me to roll down my window, and I did. She said, "Are you married yet?" I answered that I was not, she said, "Good. Don't do it."

Money was not the problem. She married him for money, and he had it, but he also had a Nabal type of a spirit about him.

Parents, you better be thinking of more than just money when it comes to advising your child on a potential mate.

I am as adamant as anyone about people working and providing, especially young men for the young ladies that they marry. But that is not the whole story, it is not the end all be all of marriage. Abigail had a very *rich* provider...who was also a very *poor* husband.

It is important for parents to be honest about their own children when it comes time for them to marry
1 Samuel 25:3 *Now the name of the man was Nabal...*

I am utterly intrigued by this man's name and how he came by it. Names today normally have very little significance to them. But in Bible times parents would often wait for a year or more to name a child, and then they would

174

name the child according to what they saw in him or the hopes they had for him.

Nabal's parents named him Nabal, which means "fool."

What must Nabal have been like even as a child!

Here is the result of that. When it came time for Abigail to marry, she knew very clearly what Nabal's parents saw in him. Once again, she probably still had very little choice in the matter, but there is a lesson to be learned here. Girls, put yourself in this situation:

A guy walks in to church right before service, and I mean a handsome guy. You saw him drive in, in his brand new Corvette. He walks in, sees you, walks over and sticks out his hand and says in the most suave voice imaginable, "Hello there, it is so good to see you. My name is Fool..."

How many of you changed your opinion of him from the time you first saw him until he told you his name? You are now likely sitting there thinking, "Man, there has got to be some bad reason for a parent to name this dude 'Fool.' I think I'll just recommend this guy over to Sally..."

Moms and dads, let me say something that may take a bit of digesting for you. If your son or daughter is not going to make a suitable mate, then you need to warn any potential mates of that fact.

The great Jonathan Edwards had a young man come to him seeking his daughter's hand in marriage. The preacher told the young man no, breaking his heart. Then he explained why. His daughter was not living for the Lord, and thus would not make a good mate for him.

Now that takes character!

But that is not what usually happens, is it. What I am about to say is not an easy thing to say, and I do not take any joy in saying it, but it needs to be said.

What usually happens is that parents with a wayward child, when they see a good young person start to show

175

interest in their child, get all excited because they feel like the good young person will help their own child to be good once a relationship is established. And there may well be some loving parents right now who are bristling inside at what I am saying, because you are thinking of your own kid, and you want the best for your own kid! Your kid means more to you than other kids.

But let me ask you a question, what if the shoe was on the other foot? What if your kid was the good kid, and some wayward kid started pursuing your child, and that kid's parents knew that their son or daughter was into drugs or pornography or perversion? What if they knew all that, but they did not say anything, and your child ended up married to their child, and then all of that came out in the marriage? How happy would you be then if the shoe was on that foot?

Parents, I hope none of you ever have to go through that. I hope I never have to go through it. But my own three kids have heard me say this to them, "If you decide to go live like the devil, I am not going to cover for you to try and get you a good mate. If you want me to tell a potential mate that you are a godly person worth marrying, then you better actually BE a godly person worth marrying!"

Parents, if you want honesty about a potential mate for your child, then be willing to be honest about your own child.

The fact that a person has an excellent family background does not mean that he is going to be excellent himself

1 Samuel 25:3b... *and he was of the house of Caleb.*

That little phrase at the end of verse three does not advance the narrative of the story in any way. It does not change the narrative of the story in any way. It does not apply to the narrative of the story in any way. You could have substituted any name at all (Abraham, Job, Isaac,

Korah, Dathan, Abiram, Pharaoh, Bob) and it would not affect what happened here.

So why is it here? There is no filler material in Scripture; there must be a reason.

There is, and it deals with marriage.

Caleb is one of the heroes of Scripture. Caleb was a spiritual giant. Nabal was from one of the most respectable families of all time. But the fact that a person has an excellent family background does not mean that he or she is going to be excellent himself!

When Abigail got married, she married Nabal, not the family history of Nabal and not Caleb himself. When you are considering a spouse, yes, the family ought to be considered. When you marry a person, you are marrying into a family. And I do not mean to be unkind in the least, but there are some really great kids out there that I will never let within a country mile of any of my three, just because of their family!

It matters to me whether or not a potential mother-in-law for one of my children is a psychopath.

It matters to me whether or not a potential father-in-law for one of my children is as unstable as water.

It matters to me whether or not a potential brother or sister-in-law for one of my children is a criminal thug.

It matters to me when I see a good kid who has learned from mama and daddy to bounce from church to church every time there is the slightest hint of trouble, because I know he or she will carry that idea with them into adulthood and marriage.

The family a person comes from ought to at least be considered when it comes to choosing a mate. But the family, even if they are fantastic, does not mean that the potential mate is. I mentioned that there are some kids I will probably not let marry mine because of the families they are from. But the opposite is also true. There are many very good families who have produced some very bad kids, and I will not let a child of mine marry a bad person just because they come from a good family!

This happened to Abigail. I do not know for sure what her parents were thinking, but it is possible that Abigail's mom and dad may have agreed to the marriage because Nabal was from such a fine, godly, upstanding family. If that is the calculation they made, then they blew it, big time. The fact that a person has an excellent family background does not mean that he or she is going to be excellent him or herself!

Abraham and Sarah were a family that God Himself approved of. But would any of you fathers let your daughter marry Ishmael? Would you let your daughter marry his nephew, Lot?

Noah was so righteous God spared him and his family when He destroyed everyone else on earth. But would you let your daughter marry his son Ham?

I know a man who pastored a solid church for years. But his daughters grew up to be reprobates. I am sure not letting my son marry any of his daughters just because he was a pastor!

The fact that a person has an excellent family background does not mean that he or she is going to be excellent him or herself!

All of these first three are things that ought to be considered before a marriage takes place. Now let's turn our attention to issues within a marriage.

Having a big mouth will definitely make you a marriage breaker

1 Samuel 25:4 *And David heard in the wilderness that Nabal did shear his sheep.* **5** *And David sent out ten young men, and David said unto the young men, Get you up to Carmel, and go to Nabal, and greet him in my name:* **6**

And thus shall ye say to him that liveth in prosperity, Peace be both to thee, and peace be to thine house, and peace be unto all that thou hast. **7** *And now I have heard that thou hast shearers: now thy shepherds which were with us, we hurt them not, neither was there ought missing unto them, all the while they were in Carmel.* **8** *Ask thy young men, and they will shew thee. Wherefore let the young men find favour in thine eyes: for we come in a good day: give, I pray thee, whatsoever cometh to thine hand unto thy servants, and to thy son David.* **9** *And when David's young men came, they spake to Nabal according to all those words in the name of David, and ceased.* **10** *And Nabal answered David's servants, and said, Who is David? and who is the son of Jesse? there be many servants now a days that break away every man from his master.* **11** *Shall I then take my bread, and my water, and my flesh that I have killed for my shearers, and give it unto men, whom I know not whence they be?* **12** *So David's young men turned their way, and went again, and came and told him all those sayings.*

Let me explain the unique thing happening in this passage, since it is a very unfamiliar custom to us today. What David and his men were asking was not at all out of the ordinary. A man's wealth in those days was primarily in flocks and herds. But that means that thieves and robbers could wipe a man out just by stealing his animals, and they often did. A man could go bankrupt overnight just at the hands of one band of rustlers.

Because of that, it became a custom for armed good guys to watch after flocks in the wilderness and keep the flocks and the shepherds safe. Then when shearing time came, the time when the owner of the animals made all of his money, the people that had kept them safe would send to him and say, "We're the ones who kept your animals safe." The owner would then check with his shepherds, and when they verified that fact, he would then pay them for what they had done. All David was asking for was the customary paycheck that he and his men had rightfully earned.

But Nabal...Nabal had a big mouth. He did not just politely refuse; that would have been bad enough, but it certainly would not have put his life and the lives of his family at risk. No, Nabal just had to use this opportunity to run his big mouth.

1 Samuel 25:10 *And Nabal answered David's servants, and said, Who is David? and who is the son of Jesse? there be many servants now a days that break away every man from his master.* **11** *Shall I then take my bread, and my water, and my flesh that I have killed for my shearers, and give it unto men, whom I know not whence they be?*

May I have the liberty to put this in modern terms that will sort of tell you how all of this came across to David?

"David?!? I don't know no stinking snot nosed brat named David. Oh, wait, you mean that pathetic little puke that Saul is after? You tell the <u>boy</u> he ain't getting nothin' from me!"

Now put yourself in the place of David. You have six hundred armed men at your disposal. You have been running from Saul, you have had multiple chances to kill him, but you have not been allowed to even touch him because he is the Lord's anointed, he is the king. You are frustrated beyond belief. And then this happens.

How do you react? Oh, yeah...

Nabal has a big mouth, and he does not mind running it. But doing so did not help his marriage; in fact, it nearly destroyed it. If it had not been for his amazing wife, it would have destroyed it.

Sir, ma'am, if you have a big mouth, for the sake of your marriage, shut it. People with a big mouth will either damage their marriage, or destroy their marriage, or they will get their children so angry that their children go wrong, or they will get someone else so furious that they come against the home like David did. There is not one thing positive in the world that ever comes from having a big mouth and running it.

Look what happened:

1 Samuel 25:12 *So David's young men turned their way, and went again, and came **and told him all those sayings.***

Imagine that scene, when the young men told David all of the vile things Nabal had said.

Proverbs 29:11 *A fool uttereth all his mind: but a wise man keepeth it in till afterwards.*

Ecclesiastes 5:3 *...a fool's voice is known by multitude of words.*

You know that loud, obnoxious person at any family celebration or work party? That is a person that some spouse somewhere regrets having married.

Gracious Abigail had to be absolutely mortified when she found out how her husband had flapped his big yap. That kind of thing does nothing to make a spouse love you. If you want to be a marriage maker, learn to not have a big mouth. Learn to not be abrasive and rude and loud and obnoxious.

If you cannot be reasonable when speaking to people, you are going to be a marriage breaker

1 Samuel 25:14 *But one of the young men told Abigail, Nabal's wife, saying, Behold, David sent messengers out of the wilderness to salute our master; and he railed on them. 15 But the men were very good unto us, and we were not hurt, neither missed we any thing, as long as we were conversant with them, when we were in the fields: 16 They were a wall unto us both by night and day, all the while we were with them keeping the sheep. 17 Now therefore know and consider what thou wilt do; for evil is*

181

determined against our master, and against all his household: for **he is such a son of Belial, that a man cannot speak to him.**

I have a very, very good friend that did not start out as a good friend, not at all. In fact, our very first conversation was by phone, and it was over an issue which we were on polar opposite sides of. I found out years later what happened before he ever called me. Before he called me, he called a mutual friend and asked him one question, "Is Brother Wagner a reasonable man?"

Our mutual friend said, "Yes, he is."

He called, brought up the very touchy issue, and we spoke about it, very reasonably on both sides, for probably an hour. We did not end up agreeing, but we did end up as friends!

There is nowhere in the world that the ability to be reasonable when speaking to people is more important than in marriage. Abigail found herself married to a man who was such a jerk that even people who were on his side thought he was a jerk! And if they, men, had trouble speaking to him, how hard must it have been for a woman, Abigail!

Sir, ma'am, there is nothing impressive about being a horse's rear end. When someone speaks to you, especially your spouse, have enough character to hold a reasonable conversation.

And by the way, some of the most unreasonable horse's patooties are men who claim to be following the Bible. Sir, nowhere in the Bible are you given instruction or permission to speak to your wife like she is a child. I feel very sorry for women who end up with husbands like that. Aquilla and Priscilla taught Apollos together. The Song of Solomon groom and bride spoke lovingly, tenderly, and respectfully to each other. Sir, if you misuse the Bible to justify being mean and condescending to your wife when

182

you speak to her, let me tell you what you are doing, you are preparing her nicely to be taken away from you by some other man who knows better.

A marriage maker knows that even though there can be no secrets in marriage, not every moment is the right moment to say something

1 Samuel 25:18 *Then Abigail made haste, and took two hundred loaves, and two bottles of wine, and five sheep ready dressed, and five measures of parched corn, and an hundred clusters of raisins, and two hundred cakes of figs, and laid them on asses.* **19** *And she said unto her servants, Go on before me; behold, I come after you.* ***But she told not her husband Nabal.***

How horrible! A wife keeping a secret from her husband! Now wait just a minute, the story does not end there. But before we go on, let me ask some questions.

What was about to happen to Nabal? He was about to be killed.

How would Nabal have responded if Abigail had asked for permission to go take the stuff to David? Bad, really bad.

So, in doing what she did, she took the only course possible to save the life of her sorry husband! You know what? If I were her, I would not have done that. I would have let David come. But before he got there I would have put all the servants behind me, way out in the yard, and I would have put on a sign board that said, "We're not the one you are looking for. Mr. Fool is in that house, right over there."

Abigail was nicer than that, though. "But she kept a secret!" No, she just waited till the right time to say what needed to be said. Keep reading and you will understand.

20 *And it was so, as she rode on the ass, that she came down by the covert of the hill, and, behold, David and* *his men came down against her; and she met them.* **21** *Now David had said, Surely in vain have I kept all that this fellow hath in the wilderness, so that nothing was missed of all that pertained unto him: and he hath requited me evil for good.* **22** *So and more also do God unto the enemies of David, if I leave of all that pertain to him by the morning light any that pisseth against the wall.* **23** *And when Abigail saw David, she hasted, and lighted off the ass, and fell before David on her face, and bowed herself to the ground,* **24** *And fell at his feet, and said, Upon me, my lord, upon me let this iniquity be: and let thine handmaid, I pray thee, speak in thine audience, and hear the words of thine handmaid.* **25** *Let not my lord, I pray thee, regard this man of Belial, even Nabal: for as his name is, so is he; Nabal is his name, and folly is with him: but I thine handmaid saw not the young men of my lord, whom thou didst send.* **26** *Now therefore, my lord, as the LORD liveth, and as thy soul liveth, seeing the LORD hath withholden thee from coming to shed blood, and from avenging thyself with thine own hand, now let thine enemies, and they that seek evil to my lord, be as Nabal.* **27** *And now this blessing which thine handmaid hath brought unto my lord, let it even be given unto the young men that follow my lord.* **28** *I pray thee, forgive the trespass of thine handmaid: for the LORD will certainly make my lord a sure house; because my lord fighteth the battles of the LORD, and evil hath not been found in thee all thy days.* **29** *Yet a man is risen to pursue thee, and to seek thy soul: but the soul of my lord shall be bound in the bundle of life with the LORD thy God; and the souls of thine enemies, them shall he sling out, as out of the middle of a sling.* **30** *And it shall come to pass, when the LORD shall have done to my lord according to all the good that he hath spoken concerning thee, and shall have appointed thee ruler over Israel;* **31** *That this shall be no grief unto thee, nor offence of heart unto my lord, either that thou hast shed blood causeless, or that my lord hath avenged*

184

*himself: but when the LORD shall have dealt well with my lord, then remember thine handmaid. 32 And David said to Abigail, Blessed be the LORD God of Israel, which sent thee this day to meet me: 33 And blessed be thy advice, and blessed be thou, which hast kept me this day from coming to shed blood, and from avenging myself with mine own hand. 34 For in very deed, as the LORD God of Israel liveth, which hath kept me back from hurting thee, except thou hadst hasted and come to meet me, surely there had not been left unto Nabal by the morning light any that pisseth against the wall. 35 So David received of her hand that which she had brought him, and said unto her, Go up in peace to thine house; see, I have hearkened to thy voice, and have accepted thy person. 36 And Abigail came to Nabal; and, behold, he held a feast in his house, like the feast of a king; and Nabal's heart was merry within him, for **he was very drunken**: wherefore she told him nothing, less or more, until the morning light. 37 But it came to pass in the morning, when the wine was gone out of Nabal, **and his wife had told him these things**, that his heart died within him, and he became as a stone.*

This ought to help you understand why Abigail did not tell him the night before! Nabal, her idiot husband, was already in the process of getting stone drunk. Does a drunk think rationally? No. Telling him the night before would have accomplished nothing good, nothing at all. But she did tell him. She told him the next morning when he sobered up.

A marriage maker knows that even though there can be no secrets in marriage, not every moment is the right moment to say something.

Sir, ma'am, be careful of what you say, but also be careful of when you say it.

Ma'am, if your husband works a brutal job all day to put food on the table, thirty seconds after he comes home

185

from work might not be the best time to tell him that you are upset with him for not taking the trash out before he left at 5:00 a.m.

Sir, if your wife has come home crying because her boss chewed her out, that might not be the best time to say "Hey, Babe, have you gained some weight lately?" In fact, there really is no good time for that one...

If there is a problem in your marriage that needs to be dealt with, carefully choose a quiet time and place. Abigail had enough sense to do just that!

A person who drinks is engaging in serious marriage breaking behavior

1 Samuel 25:36 *And Abigail came to Nabal; and, behold, he held a feast in his house, like the feast of a king; and Nabal's heart was merry within him, **for he was very drunken**: wherefore she told him nothing, less or more, until the morning light.*

Nabal, the marriage breaker, was a drinker.

It is amazing that such a thing even has to be argued about in our day. There really is no argument, there is just a fact; drinking alcohol is marriage-breaking type of behavior.

Not everyone who drinks will end up divorced, but everyone who drinks is engaging in behavior that is harmful to a home rather than helpful to a home. Everyone who drinks is moving toward the destruction of a home rather than toward the building of a home. Pick a category, any category, and I defy you to find me one category in which drinking alcohol is not harmful to a home!

How about financially? Is it not obvious that alcohol both costs money and is also addictive which makes it cost even more? An average price for a twenty-four pack of beer is $24 and average price for a twenty-four pack of soda is $6. Same exact fluid ounces, but look at the price difference! A gallon of tea can be made for less than a

186

dollar. A gallon of vodka, though? That will set you back up to $130, one hundred and thirty times more expensive than tea, for the exact same amount of liquid.

How about mentally? Every time a person drinks, it kills brain cells. It makes a husband or wife dumber, not smarter.

How about your breath? Does anyone think that beer breath smells better than minty breath?

How about your judgment? Does drinking make a husband or wife more sound in the judgment or less?

How about the ol' gut? What is better, ladies, a set of ripped abs or a big ol' beer gut?

Do people end up at the homeless shelter because they drank coffee or because they drank liquor?

Do people get DUIs for beer or for tea?

I have counseled scores and scores of homes that were falling apart because of alcohol, but I have never counseled a single home falling apart because of coffee, tea, milk, or soda.

Nabal had a great wife, an amazing wife, and yet he put his lips to the bottle and destroyed his home. Young people, boys and girls, if you want a good marriage down the line, you better make up your mind now to never let a drop of alcohol cross your lips, ever.

A marriage maker really is serious about the whole "till death us do part" thing

1 Samuel 25:37 *But it came to pass in the morning, when the wine was gone out of Nabal, and his wife had told him these things, that his heart died within him, and he became as a stone.* **38** *And it came to pass about ten days after, that the LORD smote Nabal, that he died.* **39** *And when David heard that Nabal was dead, he said, Blessed be the LORD, that hath pleaded the cause of my reproach from the hand of Nabal, and hath kept his servant from evil: for the*

LORD hath returned the wickedness of Nabal upon his own head. And David sent and communed with Abigail, to take her to him to wife. **40** *And when the servants of David were come to Abigail to Carmel, they spake unto her, saying, David sent us unto thee, to take thee to him to wife.* **41** *And she arose, and bowed herself on her face to the earth, and said, Behold, let thine handmaid be a servant to wash the feet of the servants of my lord.* **42** *And Abigail hasted, and arose, and rode upon an ass, with five damsels of hers that went after her; and she went after the messengers of David, and became his wife.*

Abigail, beautiful smart Abigail, was married to a churlish and evil man. But please pay very close attention to the last point. Despite how bad he was, she stayed with him till death did them part. In fact, please notice this, she stayed with him even after he had a stroke and became incapacitated. That is what it means when it says that his heart died within him and he became as a stone.

Husbands, wives, please get this. Even a stroke, or heart attack, or paralysis, or loss of limbs, or any other tragedy can be overcome. You can stay, you can make it work. You made a vow; keep your vow. Stay for them like you would want them staying for you. Abigail stayed for her worthless husband, while many people who call themselves Christians will not even stay for very good and godly spouses when a tragedy hits.

It was not until after he died, ten days later, that Abigail moved on.

This was a union between a marriage maker and a marriage breaker. It was one of those things that preachers hate to see, where a good person somehow ends up with a very bad person.

If you are not married yet, you better choose very, very carefully.

If you are married, you better make sure that you, whether a man or woman, have the attitude of Abigail, not that of Nabal.

If you are married and you see in yourself the attitude and traits of Nabal, you better fix it, now. God Himself stepped in on behalf of Abigail, and He did so by killing Nabal. Please do not make it necessary for Him to do so to you.

Chapter 14
No Marriage Ever Started Worse Than Ours

"Greetings, and may the Lord be with you. Your study of marriage has brought you to many different places and people in the precious Word of God. But I am certain that your studies have never yet taken you quite as far afield as this one will.

"What I mean by that is this, no marriage ever began under worst auspices than ours. It is with the greatest of shame that I think back on my wickedness and all that it cost.

"Marriage is a sacred thing, a union between one man and one woman and God Himself. I desecrated that picture, twisted, warped, and ruined it. The only people that I made happy with the way I started my marriage was the devil himself and all of the enemies of God.

"Yet, in spite of all of that, marriage is still marriage, and a marriage vow is still a vow.

"My wife and I, despite our horrific beginning, made our marriage work and made it last. We may not serve as much of an instruction manual for those who have had the good sense to start things right, but we can certainly be a teaching tool for those who have started their homes wrong.

"Who are we? We are the couple who made their marriage work in spite of the fact that no marriage ever started worse than ours; we are David and Bathsheba."

2 Samuel 11:1 *And it came to pass, after the year was expired, at the time when kings go forth to battle, that David sent Joab, and his servants with him, and all Israel; and they destroyed the children of Ammon, and besieged Rabbah. But David tarried still at Jerusalem. 2 And it came to pass in an eveningtide, that David arose from off his bed, and walked upon the roof of the king's house: and from the roof he saw a woman washing herself; and the woman was very beautiful to look upon. 3 And David sent and enquired after the woman. And one said, Is not this Bathsheba, the daughter of Eliam, the wife of Uriah the Hittite? 4 And David sent messengers, and took her; and she came in unto him, and he lay with her; for she was purified from her uncleanness: and she returned unto her house. 5 And the woman conceived, and sent and told David, and said, I am with child. 6 And David sent to Joab, saying, Send me Uriah the Hittite. And Joab sent Uriah to David. 7 And when Uriah was come unto him, David demanded of him how Joab did, and how the people did, and how the war prospered. 8 And David said to Uriah, Go down to thy house, and wash thy feet. And Uriah departed out of the king's house, and there followed him a mess of meat from the king. 9 But Uriah slept at the door of the king's house with all the servants of his lord, and went not down to his house. 10 And when they had told David, saying, Uriah went not down unto his house, David said unto Uriah, Camest thou not from thy journey? why then didst thou not go down unto thine house? 11 And Uriah said unto David, The ark, and Israel, and Judah, abide in tents; and my lord Joab, and the servants of my lord, are encamped in the open fields; shall I then go into mine house, to eat and to drink, and to lie with my wife? as thou* *livest, and as thy soul liveth, I will not do this thing.* **12** *And David said to Uriah, Tarry here to day also, and to morrow I will let thee depart. So Uriah abode in Jerusalem that day, and the morrow.* **13** *And when David had called him, he did eat and drink before him; and he made him drunk: and at even he went out to lie on his bed with the servants of his lord, but went not down to his house.* **14** *And it came to pass in the morning, that David wrote a letter to Joab, and sent it by the hand of Uriah.* **15** *And he wrote in the letter, saying, Set ye Uriah in the forefront of the hottest battle, and retire ye from him, that he may be smitten, and die.* **16** *And it came to pass, when Joab observed the city, that he assigned Uriah unto a place where he knew that valiant men were.* **17** *And the men of the city went out, and fought with Joab: and there fell some of the people of the servants of David; and Uriah the Hittite died also.* **18** *Then Joab sent and told David all the things concerning the war;* **19** *And charged the messenger, saying, When thou hast made an end of telling the matters of the war unto the king,* **20** *And if so be that the king's wrath arise, and he say unto thee, Wherefore approached ye so nigh unto the city when ye did fight? knew ye not that they would shoot from the wall?* **21** *Who smote Abimelech the son of Jerubbesheth? did not a woman cast a piece of a millstone upon him from the wall, that he died in Thebez? why went ye nigh the wall? then say thou, Thy servant Uriah the Hittite is dead also.* **22** *So the messenger went, and came and shewed David all that Joab had sent him for.* **23** *And the messenger said unto David, Surely the men prevailed against us, and came out unto us into the field, and we were upon them even unto the entering of the gate.* **24** *And the shooters shot from off the wall upon thy servants; and some of the king's servants be dead, and thy servant Uriah the Hittite is dead also.* **25** *Then David said unto the messenger, Thus shalt thou say unto Joab, Let not this thing displease thee, for the sword devoureth one as well as* *another: make thy battle more strong against the city, and overthrow it: and encourage thou him.* **26** *And when the wife of Uriah heard that Uriah her husband was dead, she mourned for her husband.* **27** *And when the mourning was past, David sent and fetched her to his house, and she became his wife, and bare him a son. But the thing that David had done displeased the LORD.*

The account of David and Bathsheba makes up the darkest and most sordid affair in the life of one of the greatest men of God who has ever lived, David. David humbly served God as a shepherd out in the field, heroically slew Goliath with a sling and a stone, and then hardened his soul against all that was right when he took Bathsheba and murdered her husband.

It is right and proper for us to examine just how incredibly wicked this sin was.

Adultery is never right.

Covering up sin is never right.

Murder is never right.

David paid a very, very high price for all of that wrong.

Those things should be looked at, they should be studied, they should be preached against.

But the story does not end there. I have heard more messages than I can possibly count about David's great sin with Bathsheba. But I have never, ever heard so much as a single message nor read a single book about the marriage that followed.

For everything that David and Bathsheba did that was so very, incredibly wrong, there is one thing that they did that was right. They moved past their sin and made their marriage work anyway.

I know that in saying and preaching and writing this I run two risks. One, there will be some who react in horror, there will be some who believe that David and Bathsheba should have ended their marriage since it started wrong, and those people will tune me out right away. I hope they choose not to, because they are wrong. One sin is never fixed by committing another sin!

Two, there will be sinful and carnal people who perhaps decide to do wrong, reasoning that they can take their medicine, be forgiven, and then enjoy what they wanted anyway. People like that cannot be helped for one simple reason–they are lost.

Anyone who believes that way and behaves that way has clearly never become the new creature in Christ that 2 Corinthians 5:17 speaks of! Their old desires and old ways are still very much alive, and, therefore, they are still very much spiritually dead.

With those risks addressed, let's see if we can begin to help some folks. You see, in a perfect world this chapter of the book would not be necessary, but this is not a perfect world. This is a sin cursed world, and because of that, people sometimes do some very wrong and foolish things. Some of you may have started your marriage off in an unbelievably wrong way. If you did, this chapter may well help you more than any other one in this entire book.

The beginning to overcome

David and Bathsheba first of all had to overcome a beginning that was rooted in lust alone.

2 Samuel 11:2 *And it came to pass in an eveningtide, that David arose from off his bed, and walked upon the roof of the king's house: and from the roof he **saw** a woman washing herself; and the woman was **very beautiful** to look upon.*

From the very beginning everything in this "relationship" had no real content to it at all, it was just animalistic desire. A relationship began under those auspices will inevitably run into trouble at some point. What happens when old age sets in and beauty begins to fade? What happens if an accident occurs marring one's natural attractiveness?

Physical desire is important, please do not misunderstand me and think that I do not know that.

I remember a friend many years ago who was set up with a girl by some powerful religious figures in his life. These "popish powers that be" had determined that the two of them would have a long life of serving the Lord together as man and wife. But, to be as kind as I possibly can, the girl was extremely unattractive! I am talking about "even the tide wouldn't take her out" kind of unattractive.

My friend stopped me one day, with a worried look on his face and literally wringing his hands, asked me, "Do you think it is important to be attracted to someone before you marry them?"

I looked directly in his eyes, smiled, and then literally shouted, "YEEEEEESSSSSSSSSSSSS!"

He married someone else. He and his wife and kids are serving the Lord to this day.

There is someone for most everyone, including the lady I described above. Someone will no doubt find her attractive! My point is, all through the Bible, men noticed the natural attractiveness of the women they chose to marry. But if the marriage is based simply on that natural lust, it is being built on a very shaky foundation indeed.

David and Bathsheba also had to overcome a beginning that was brought about by an unplanned pregnancy.

2 Samuel 11:5 *And the woman conceived, and sent and told David, and said, I am with child.*

Had it not been for the pregnancy, this may well have just been a one night stand, a wicked deed that never led to a marriage. But with the pregnancy, there was now a pressure, and that pressure led to a marriage. That is not how people who are wise want to begin a marriage!

They then had to overcome a beginning that was brought about by the murder of a friend.

2 Samuel 11:6 *And David sent to Joab, saying, Send me Uriah the Hittite. And Joab sent Uriah to David.* **7** *And when Uriah was come unto him, David demanded of him how Joab did, and how the people did, and how the war prospered.* **8** *And David said to Uriah, Go down to thy house, and wash thy feet. And Uriah departed out of the king's house, and there followed him a mess of meat from the king.* **9** *But Uriah slept at the door of the king's house with all the servants of his lord, and went not down to his house.* **10** *And when they had told David, saying, Uriah went not down unto his house, David said unto Uriah, Camest thou not from thy journey? why then didst thou not go down unto thine house?* **11** *And Uriah said unto David, The ark, and Israel, and Judah, abide in tents; and my lord Joab, and the servants of my lord, are encamped in the open fields; shall I then go into mine house, to eat and to drink, and to lie with my wife? as thou livest, and as thy soul liveth, I will not do this thing.* **12** *And David said to Uriah, Tarry here to day also, and to morrow I will let thee depart. So Uriah abode in Jerusalem that day, and the morrow.* **13** *And when David had called him, he did eat and drink before him; and he made him drunk: and at even he went out to lie on his bed with the servants of his lord, but went not down to his house.* **14** *And it came to pass in the morning, that David wrote a letter to Joab, and sent it by the hand of Uriah.* **15** *And he wrote in the letter, saying, Set ye Uriah in the forefront of the hottest battle, and retire ye from him, that he may be smitten, and die.*

Uriah was not just some random guy. He was one of David's handful of most loyal and skilled fighters, those who stayed close to him night and day! They were called his "mighty men." Uriah was a man who had quite literally risked his own life for David time and time again. He loved David; he would have died for David at a moment's notice.

David had a friend, a really good friend, a loyal friend, and he murdered him to take his wife. This was how the marriage of David and Bathsheba began!

They also had to overcome a beginning where their sin caused the death of their baby.

2 Samuel 12:13 *And David said unto Nathan, I have sinned against the LORD. And Nathan said unto David, The LORD also hath put away thy sin; thou shalt not die.* **14** *Howbeit, because by this deed thou hast given great occasion to the enemies of the LORD to blaspheme, the child also that is born unto thee shall surely die.*

Do you see now why I say that there has never been a marriage that started as badly as this one did? Lust, adultery, murder, the death of a baby, if there was ever a marriage that started so badly that you would never ever give it even a chance to survive, this was it!

You who perhaps started your own marriage wrong, be encouraged, you did not start it *this* wrong! But the good news is, despite the bad beginning to overcome, they did overcome it and went on to have a long and successful marriage.

The basis of that overcoming

I mentioned at the very beginning of this chapter that there are people who believe that any marriage that has started wrong should be ended. They actually say that a divorce should take place, or that at the very least people should stay married but never sleep together again.

David and Bathsheba did not take that approach, and they were right to not take that approach. God still hates divorce according to Malachi 2:16, and one sin never cleansed another sin! David figured this out, and we can see much of his reasoning in the two penitential psalms that he wrote after his great sin, Psalm 38 and 51.

Psalm 38:17 *For I am ready to halt, and my sorrow is continually before me.* **18** *For I will declare mine iniquity;* ***I will be sorry for my sin.***

The first basis for overcoming the bad beginning was repentance. David was genuinely sorry for what he had done wrong, not just for the consequences that followed.

That repentance dove tails into the second basis for overcoming the bad beginning, found in the next of David's penitential Psalms:

Psalm 51:1 *Have mercy upon me, O God, according to thy lovingkindness: according unto the multitude of thy tender mercies blot out my transgressions.* **2** *Wash me throughly from mine iniquity, and cleanse me from my sin.*

Twice David mentioned his need for mercy. That is very significant. It tells us that if there was anything he could have *done* to fix things, anything like "dissolving his new marriage since it started wrong," he would have done so. But he knew that nothing he could do would fix things, all he could do therefore was just fall on the mercies of God!

He continued into the third basis:

Psalm 51:7 *Purge me with hyssop, and I shall be* ***clean****: wash me, and I shall be* ***whiter than snow****.*

Psalm 51:10 *Create in me a* ***clean*** *heart, O God; and renew a* ***right*** *spirit within me.*

Clean...whiter than snow...clean...right.

And every bit of it happened without David divorcing Bathsheba! Every bit of it happened as a work of God. Every bit of it happened because Jesus Christ was going to die on Calvary to pay for what David had done! Every bit of it happened as an act of grace, not an act of works. Every bit of it happened because the truth of 1 John 1:7 is not just a New Testament truth, it is a forever truth.

1 John 1:7b *...and the blood of Jesus Christ his Son cleanseth us from all sin.*

What David did could not be fixed by his works! God had to step in and cleanse him. And He did. David repented, God forgave and cleansed him, and at that point divorcing Bathsheba would have just been one more sin to have to get forgiveness of.

There are sins you can commit that will have consequences that, in this lifetime, will never be taken away. The sword never did depart from David's house. A person who gets divorced and remarried cannot be a preacher or a deacon, even though he has been forgiven. But there is no such thing as a sin that can be fixed by committing another sin.

If your marriage started wrong, your basis for overcoming that beginning is not any work that you can do, your basis for overcoming that beginning is the complete forgiveness that comes from the blood of Christ! If you have repented and received forgiveness for your sin, then no matter what life-long consequences you may have to deal with, you are just as pure and your marriage is just as right as a person who did everything right from the get go!

The basics of how to overcome

I am certain that this is where interested people want to get. If you know that it is right to make your marriage work anyway, then you want to know how David and Bathsheba did it.

I believe that the Bible says a great deal about this in a very few words. We already know that David repented; let's assume that Bathsheba did the same thing. Repentance is an absolute must. So with that covered, let's look at what else they did.

First, they mourned, then moved on.

A very unique thing happens in the text, something in the grammar itself, and I believe it gives us great insight into what was actually going on in the heart and mind of Bathsheba. People for years have wondered how much of a willing role she played in all of this. Was she genuine? Was she a good wife to Uriah, a lady who was just scared of the king?

We may never know all of the answers to those questions, but I believe that the grammar of Scripture very clearly tells us that Bathsheba was genuinely broken hearted over everything that happened. Let me show you:

2 Samuel 11:26 *And when the wife of Uriah heard that Uriah her husband was dead, she **mourned** for her husband. 27 And when the **mourning** was past, David sent and fetched her to his house, and she became his wife, and bare him a son. But the thing that David had done displeased the LORD.*

The English word "mourn" appears both in verse twenty-six and twenty-seven. But they are from two completely different words in Hebrew. In verse twenty-seven, it is from the word *aybel*, and it is talking about the ritual of mourning for the dead. That was a very orchestrated thing and was often done by hired professionals.

But in the verse before that, when Bathsheba first heard of her husband's death, and it says that she mourned for him, a completely different word is used. That is from the word *sawfad*, and it means to wail and to lament. It is used in 2 Samuel 1:12 when David mourned for his best friend Jonathan. It is used in Genesis 50:10 when Joseph and the rest of his brothers mourned over the death of Jacob their father. It looks very much to me like Bathsheba was truly devastated over what they had done and over what it had cost.

David did his own mourning later as we saw in Psalm 38 and 51.

201

They mourned...then they moved on. No matter how badly your marriage started, you cannot allow yourself to mourn forever. Mourning never *fixes* the past, it simply *fixes you to* the past.

Secondly, once the marriage started, they treated each other just as well as if it had started perfectly.

2 Samuel 12:24 *And David comforted Bathsheba his wife, and went in unto her, and lay with her: and she bare a son, and he called his name Solomon: and the LORD loved him.* **25** *And he sent by the hand of Nathan the prophet; and he called his name Jedidiah, because of the LORD.*

Bathsheba sinned, yes, but she was also a broken-hearted mother. And David her husband treated her exactly as he was supposed to.

They had normal marital relations.

They produced another child.

No matter how the marriage starts, once it is started, treat each other just as well as if it had started perfectly. In fact, if your marriage started wrong, you might want to treat each other even better than people in a "normal marriage relationship," because you have more working against you than they do!

Thirdly, they were not afraid to be happy.

Notice that when David and Bathsheba produced another child, the Bible says that "The LORD loved him!" Is that what you would expect? Not if you listen to some people.

The name Solomon means "peace." It is an indication that David and Bathsheba were expecting things to go well at this point. It is an indication that they were going to allow themselves to be happy. Yes they sinned, yes Uriah was murdered, yes a baby died because of all that, but all of that had been dealt with. This was a new day, and they were holding a brand new baby! This was now a happy mama and a happy papa.

No matter how your marriage started, if you have repented and gotten forgiveness, make your current marriage work. And one of the best ways to do that is by not being afraid to be happy again! If you let him, the devil will make sure that you are consumed with guilt for the rest of your life over what you have done. If that ever starts to happen, go read Isaiah 53 and ask yourself one question: is what Jesus suffered punishment enough for what I did? Since the answer is yes, let it go and do not be afraid to be happy again.

The benefits of overcoming

Please understand that the devil is just as interested in destroying marriages that did not start right as he is in destroying marriages that did start right. The union of one man and one woman is still an ugly thing to him, and he hates it. But no matter how your marriage started, there are benefits to repenting and then making your marriage work.

For starters, children produced by a marriage that started wrong are still just as precious and still as full of potential as children produced by a marriage that started right.

2 Samuel 12:24 *And David comforted Bathsheba his wife, and went in unto her, and lay with her: and she bare a son, and he called his name Solomon: and the LORD loved him.*

David and Bathsheba stayed together, they made it work and look at the result. This baby boy of theirs, Solomon, do you know what he did? Maybe these words will help: Proverbs, Ecclesiastes, Song of Solomon.

He wrote those books.

How many of you are helped, even today, when you read the words:

Proverbs 3:5 *Trust in the LORD with all thine heart; and lean not unto thine own understanding.* **6** *In all thy ways acknowledge him, and he shall direct thy paths.*

Solomon wrote that.

How many of you are helped, even today, when you read the words:

Ecclesiastes 12:13 *Let us hear the conclusion of the whole matter: Fear God, and keep his commandments: for this is the whole duty of man.*

Solomon wrote that.

When you get help for your marriage out of the Song of Solomon, Solomon wrote that. David and Bathsheba stayed together, they made it work, and the son that was born to them became a blessing even to us today!

The second thing to consider is that marriages that start wrong often produce a stronger marital bond than even marriages that were started right, because there is a common heartbreak that helps them to endure whatever else may come.

David had more than one wife. One wife that he had would have seemed to be perfect, and the marriage started just right, it even had her father's approval on it. That would be the marriage between David and Michal. But that marriage split up! Despite its good beginning, the very first time they had even a hint of trouble, they broke up. But look at this:

1 Kings 1:15 *And Bathsheba went in unto the king into the chamber: and the king was very old...*

Bathsheba stayed with David till the day he died! Michal flaked out at the very first hint of trouble. Bathsheba stayed through the death of a baby, the stealing of the kingdom by a stepson, wars, judgment, and disease. She stayed through it all.

Marriages that start wrong often produce a stronger marital bond than even marriages that were started right, because there is a common heartbreak that helps them to endure whatever else may come.

Sir, ma'am, you may have started your marriage off in the worst way possible. I have seen people come through my church who did that. In every case, I have not prayed for them to fail because they started their marriage wrong. In every case I have prayed for them to succeed anyway! No matter how you started, you have a responsibility to make it work. David and Bathsheba did, and if they did, you can too.

Chapter 15
Married without Children

"Greetings, people of the Lord. It is our honor to communicate with you by means of letter. Our marriage was a good one, one that lasted for very, very, many years, till death did us part.

"When most people marry, there are certain expectations that they bring with them into the marriage. One of those very common expectations is that of having children! My wife and I certainly desired them, as did almost every married couple around us.

"The difference was, others had them, and we did not.

"This was, more than you in your time and culture can imagine, a horrible, horrible thing. For a husband and wife to go without children was not just a heartbreak to them, but to everyone who looked on; it was regarded as a sign that God Himself was somehow displeased with them.

"My wife was a good and a godly wife, and I served the Lord with all my might and loved Him with all my heart! There was no reason for us to be without children, and yet we were.

"Now, very, very many years into our marriage, when we were both well past child bearing age, my wife miraculously had a son! But that is a story for another day. For this day, and given that you are studying marriage, the thing that you need to know is that my wife and I spent our entire marriage up until the very last few days in a house with an empty nursery.

"Who are we? Why, we are the couple that you could describe as 'Married Without Children.' We are Zacharias and Elisabeth."

Luke 1:5 *There was in the days of Herod, the king of Judaea, a certain priest named Zacharias, of the course of Abia: and his wife was of the daughters of Aaron, and her name was Elisabeth.* **6** *And they were both righteous before God, walking in all the commandments and ordinances of the Lord blameless.* **7** *And they had no child, because that Elisabeth was barren, and they both were now well stricken in years.* **8** *And it came to pass, that while he executed the priest's office before God in the order of his course,* **9** *According to the custom of the priest's office, his lot was to burn incense when he went into the temple of the Lord.* **10** *And the whole multitude of the people were praying without at the time of incense.* **11** *And there appeared unto him an angel of the Lord standing on the right side of the altar of incense.* **12** *And when Zacharias saw him, he was troubled, and fear fell upon him.* **13** *But the angel said unto him, Fear not, Zacharias: for thy prayer is heard; and thy wife Elisabeth shall bear thee a son, and thou shalt call his name John.* **14** *And thou shalt have joy and gladness; and many shall rejoice at his birth.*

There is something in the heart of a man and wife that almost invariably ends up desiring children. I have been pastoring for a very, very long time. During that time I have seen something happen over and over again. I have talked with young people and had them look me right in the eyes and say, "I'm never having kids; I don't want any." And then time after time, those kids have gotten married a few months later, and "voila," a few months after that the girl is pregnant! And the young person who swore up and down he/she never wanted kids is suddenly walking on clouds, thrilled to death, shopping for nursery stuff.

God puts this desire into the heart of people, and it is a very, very strong desire.

But that is where an unexpected and often very heart-wrenching thing often takes place. You see, I have noticed something else a great many times through the years. There will be a wicked girl, sleeping around with everything that moves, and she will produce babies like rabbits. But then there will be a good girl and a good guy who do everything right, and for some reason God does not allow them to have children. Those folks will often spend their entire married lives together, do right, grow old together, and never have kids.

And that, friends, can make a person bitter and can even put a marriage at risk.

But it does not have to. A marriage can be heaven on earth even when that overwhelming desire is not met.

A couple who understood the anguish and pressure of not having children was Zacharias and Elisabeth. For decades before the miraculous birth of John, they could not have any children. Yet they survived it, and their marriage thrived. They were marriage makers even through the heartache of not having children. Let's go through their story and see why they had such a successful marriage even through that great heartache.

This was a couple that maintained a right walk with God even while God did not give them the greatest desire of their hearts

Luke 1:5 *There was in the days of Herod, the king of Judaea, a certain priest named Zacharias, of the course* *of Abia: and his wife was of the daughters of Aaron, and her name was Elisabeth. 6 And they were both righteous before God, walking in all the commandments and ordinances of the Lord blameless.*

This couple thought enough of God to marry right, it was a believer marrying a believer, a godly man marrying a godly woman.

This couple thought enough of God to do "all" things right: *And they were both righteous before God, walking in **all** the commandments and ordinances of the Lord blameless.*

By this time in their lives, they were very old, and God had not given them the one greatest desire of their hearts, yet they still maintained a right walk with God even while God did not give them the greatest desire of their hearts! This had to be very hard for them, seeing others, good and bad, have kids and being expected to still be devoted even through heartache.

It is always hard for a godly couple to go through this. But one of the reasons that their marriage survived and thrived is because they maintained a right walk with God even while God did not give them the greatest desire of their hearts.

It is easy to maintain a right walk with God while he is giving you what you desire...not so easy when He does not! The devil uses the lack of this desire being fulfilled to play with people's minds, and to tell them that God doesn't care, and that they would be better off living for the flesh than for the Lord.

You better not listen to him. If Zacharias or Elisabeth had listened to the devil's lies on this, a very good home would have been destroyed along the way. Zacharias was a good husband! Elisabeth was a good wife! You do not give that up just because you cannot have kids! But if you do not maintain your walk with the Lord through that disappointment, you will.

This principle applies to all disappointments. In every marriage there will be things that you desperately want but cannot seem to have. Maintain a right walk with the Lord anyway, because that is the first key to maintaining your marriage! It is your foundation!

This was a couple that maintained their marriage even when one could not fulfill the desires of the other

Luke 1:7 *And they had no child, because that Elisabeth was barren...*

Oftentimes in a situation like this, it can either be a problem with the woman or with the man. But for whatever reason, God chose to let us know that in this case it was a problem with Elisabeth. In those days, for a man to be without a child, especially without a son, was just devastating. Whatever physical issue this was that Elisabeth had, it kept her from fulfilling one of Zacharias' greatest desires.

But assuming they both married about the normal time, they went through their youthful twenties, Elisabeth could not give Zacharias this great desire, but all through their youthful twenties he just stayed and loved her.

Then they went through their established thirties, Elisabeth still could not give Zacharias this great desire, but all through their established thirties he just stayed and loved her.

Then they went through their mature forties, Elisabeth still could not give Zacharias this great desire, but all through their mature forties he just stayed and loved her, even though he realized that by now, it really was getting to be almost too late.

Then they went through their "we should be grandparents by now" fifties, Elisabeth still could not give

211

Zacharias this great desire, but all through their "we should be grandparents by now" fifties, he just stayed and loved her.

Then they went through their golden-years sixties, Elisabeth still could not give Zacharias this great desire, but all through their golden-years sixties, he just stayed and loved her.

Then they went through their "where did I put my glasses and dentures seventies," and Elisabeth still could not give Zacharias this great desire, but all through their "where did I put my glasses and dentures seventies," he just stayed and loved her.

Then they get maybe into their "we better go ahead and pick out grave plot eighties," and all of a sudden they have a child!

For decade after decade after decade she could not give him his greatest desire, yet he stayed and loved and loved and stayed and stayed and loved and loved and stayed and stayed and loved and loved and stayed the entire time!

Sir, ma'am, there may be a desire in your heart, a strong one, one that for whatever reason your spouse cannot fulfill. Whatever it is, the right solution is just for you to stay and love and love and stay and stay and love and love and stay! Can you imagine the amazing times together these two had with this kind of devotion on his part? Think about it. How much did she have to love him based on how much he chose to love her!

And since they did not have kids, she had all kinds of time on her hands to show him how much she loved him back!

There was a couple in the Old Testament who went through a very similar situation, their names were Hannah and Elkanah. I want you to see what he said to her while they were going through it.

1 Samuel 1:8 *Then said Elkanah her husband to her, Hannah, why weepest thou? and why eatest thou not? and* *why is thy heart grieved?* ***am not I better to thee than ten sons?***

Do you see that? Elkanah decided that since his wife could not have kids, he would treat her so good she would be happier than if she had ten sons! And that kind of attitude from a husband to a wife was almost unheard of in those days!

But that kind of attitude is what he had and what Zacharias clearly had. It is the kind of attitude that every husband or wife ought to have when they find themselves in a situation where one of them cannot fulfill the desires of the other.

Your husband may not have it in him to be a regular Don Juan. You can only get people so far. You may get him from, "I gawt yew sum flaers outter duh feeuld" to "I got you some flowers out of the field" but you will probably not get him to a person who, in a Latin voice, with a bouquet of daisies held between his teeth somehow still manages to bend you over backwards and say, "My dear, my flower, my sweet, life has no meaning without you, and so I have picked you these flowers not to show you how beautiful they are, but to show them how beautiful you are."

Your wife may never be able to make a super model look bad.

No matter what desire they cannot fulfill, maintain that marriage, love and stay and stay and love!

This was a couple that spent their lives enjoying each other in the absence of children

Luke 1:7 *And they had no child, because that Elisabeth was barren, and they both were now well stricken in years.*

Keep what this verse says in your mind; they are both very old now, and they have no children. In fact, they are beyond child-bearing years. Now look at verse thirteen:

213

Luke 1:13 *But the angel said unto him, Fear not, Zacharias: for thy prayer is heard; and thy wife Elisabeth shall bear thee a son, and thou shalt call his name John.*

Do you know what I know from reading verse thirteen? Even though they were old, Zacharias and Elisabeth were, ahem, still enjoying each other! If Zacharias was still praying it, he and his wife were still doing it!

Many couples who for whatever reason cannot have children make a huge mistake. The mistake they make is to make intimacy a project with the purpose of producing a child. They time everything and schedule everything and it is all about getting pregnant. But as the months and years drag on with no success, that which should be a bonding experience between husband and wife actually drives a wedge between them!

Zacharias and Elisabeth clearly kept on enjoying each other.

"But they were old!" Yes, but as the old timers say, "Snow on the roof don't mean there's no fire in the stove!"

Sir, ma'am, not just in intimacy, but in everything marriage related, if you cannot have kids, make that much more sure to enjoy each other.

Go more places together.
Learn more things together.
Try more experiences together.
Enjoy each other even in the absence of children!

This was a family for whom serving others was their life
Luke 1:8 *And it came to pass, that while he executed the priest's office before God in the order of his course,*

Zacharias and Elisabeth did not have children. But what they did have were others, and they spent their time serving those others!

And even in that he showed his character. The job he did on this day was so special it could only be done once in a lifetime. He gave himself for others day after day, even when he went a lifetime with no glory and recognition! It is no wonder they did not mope and whine and get depressed; they did not have time to!

A couple that does not have children of their own will have something else–time to help others!

Maybe it is foster parenting.

Maybe it is going through the roller coaster of an adoption.

Maybe it is just becoming every kid's nana and pawpaw.

Maybe it is serving old folks.

If God has not given you kids, He HAS given you time to serve others! And please listen to someone who has been helping marriages for years, people who do that together tend to have very good marriages!

This was a husband for whom pleasing God was more important than building a legacy

Luke 1:57 *Now Elisabeth's full time came that she should be delivered; and she brought forth a son. 58 And her neighbours and her cousins heard how the Lord had shewed great mercy upon her; and they rejoiced with her. 59 And it came to pass, that on the eighth day they came to circumcise the child; and they called him Zacharias, after the name of his father. 60 And his mother answered and said, Not so; but he shall be called John. 61 And they said unto her, There is none of thy kindred that is called by this name. 62 And they made signs to his father, how he would have him called. 63 And he asked for a writing table, and wrote, saying, His name is John. And they marvelled all.*

This part of the text gives us a great deal of insight into the character of this husband. When a boy was born, it was really common for that boy to be called after his father in some way. Sometimes it would be direct, the child would

215

be given the same name, like they wanted to do here. Sometimes the boy would be given a second name that tied with the father, such as Simon Barjonas, meaning "Simon son of Jonas." Sometimes the boy would be given a prefix that did it. Bartimaues means "The son of Timmaeus."

This was about legacy.

But Zacharias was a husband for whom pleasing God was more important than building a legacy!

Sir, if you have not been able to have a child, you may be very concerned with your legacy. But Zacharias was apparently one who spent his life focusing on something more important–pleasing God. That tends to make a man a very good husband!

This was a couple for whom the question "why?" was not the dominant thing in their lives

Please let me explain this. Here is a question to begin with: were Zacharias and Elisabeth human beings with all of the normal emotions that others had? Yes.

That being the case, you know for a fact that they wondered why, and that they even asked the question from time to time. There is no question about that. But when you read their account, "why" is not even mentioned. That tells us that even though they no doubt asked it, it was not the dominant thought, the dominant emotion, the dominant thing in their lives.

Let me show you what was, out of Elisabeth's own mouth:

Luke 1:39 *And Mary arose in those days, and went into the hill country with haste, into a city of Juda; 40 And entered into the house of Zacharias, and saluted Elisabeth. 41 And it came to pass, that, when Elisabeth heard the salutation of Mary, the babe leaped in her womb; and* **Elisabeth was filled with the Holy Ghost***: 42 And she spake out with a loud voice, and said, Blessed art thou among* *women, and blessed is the fruit of thy womb.* **43** *And whence is this to me, that the mother of **my Lord** should come to me?* **44** *For, lo, as soon as the voice of thy salutation sounded in mine ears, the babe leaped in my womb for joy.* **45** *And blessed is she that believed: for there shall be a performance of those things which were told her from **the Lord**.*

"Filled with the Holy Ghost...my Lord...the Lord..." This kind of spirit does not happen overnight; it is the product of the way a life has been lived up unto that point. I am quite sure both Zacharias and Elisabeth asked why from time to time. But it is very clear that "why" was not the dominant thing in their lives.

"Whys?" are inevitable. "Whys?" are ok! Just be sure to never allow it to become the dominant thing.

It is very clear that there were several things more dominant to them. Their walk with the Lord...their relationship with each other...all of the things that really mattered.

There are going to be some very good and godly couples that want children but do not have them. That does not mean that your marriage has to struggle. May I summarize this entire chapter in one statement? The marriage of Zacharias and Elisabeth thrived because even though they longed for that third person that their family did not have, they focused on that Third Person that their family did have.

Chapter 16
The Man Who Never Quit on His Marriage
Even Though He Had Every Reason to Do So

"Greetings, people of the Lord. It is my desire to help you today through this letter, and I believe I am in a unique position to do so. Many men in the Bible were unfaithful to their wives, but I am one of the rare men whose wife cheated on him. She did so over and again, in fact, she became famous for it.

"This was devastating to our marriage.

"For my part, I faced a battle between what I was allowed to do and what I knew the Lord wanted me to do. Under the law, I was allowed to divorce my wife; I was even allowed to bring her to justice, which would have meant her death. I could have done either of those things and been well within my rights!

"But 'rights' are not always the same thing as 'right.' And in our case, I knew it was right to do the unthinkable. I did so, and it saved our marriage. Who am I? Why, I am the man who never quit on his marriage even though I had every reason to do so; I am Hosea."

The unusual call of Hosea

Hosea 1:1 *The word of the LORD that came unto Hosea, the son of Beeri, in the days of Uzziah, Jotham, Ahaz, and Hezekiah, kings of Judah, and in the days of Jeroboam the son of Joash, king of Israel.* **2** *The beginning of the word of the LORD by Hosea. And the LORD said to Hosea, Go, take unto thee a wife of whoredoms and children of whoredoms: for the land hath committed great whoredom, departing from the LORD.* **3** *So he went and took Gomer the daughter of Diblaim; which conceived, and bare him a son.*

There is no way to overemphasize just how unusual of a demand God made of the prophet Hosea in this text. God told Hosea that he was to marry a woman who was known to be promiscuous and who was known to have produced children by her fornication.

This was absolutely unheard of! In fact, this is the kind of thing that God usually had His men preach against.

Why? What purpose could there be for such a thing?

The answer is found in the people of God themselves. God's people, Israel, had been behaving toward Him like Gomer had been behaving; they had been committing spiritual fornication. They had been "cheating on God."

But they were okay with that. They were not shocked in the least by their own wicked behavior.

Enter Hosea.

When Hosea showed up one day and announced that he was married, naturally everyone wanted to know who the lucky girl was. Imagine the shock when the preacher said, "Oh, I married the local prostitute; I married Gomer." Imagine the shocked reactions!

"Hosea! You cannot marry her; she is loose and immoral! Do you know how bad this looks!?!"

"Tsk, tsk, Hosea, you should think more of God than that!"

"Hosea, don't you know better than that?"

And that gave Hosea the exact opening that God wanted him to have. It gave him the chance to say, "Are you shocked by this? Why? Is this not exactly what you have been doing to God?"

When Gomer later cheated on Hosea, it then gave him the chance to say, "And this is just like you as well. God took you to Himself even when you were wicked, He cleaned you up and took you in, and you have shown your gratitude by cheating on Him!" This was the purpose behind what God had Hosea do in marrying Gomer.

But the spiritual reason behind all of this does not change the fact that Hosea literally got married, and he loved a woman that most people would not be willing to love. As you read the book of Hosea, it is very clear that he was really attached to his wife.

And then in verse three, that attachment grew even stronger. Gomer came to her husband one day and said, "Honey, we're going to have a baby!"

That began the entire nine month wonder, seeing her belly grow, feeling the baby kick, wondering if it would be a boy or a girl.

And then the big day came, and Gomer gave Hosea a son. This was a good marriage, and Hosea loved his wife!

The unfathomable hurt of Hosea

While we are still early in chapter one, things are, amazingly, going well in the marriage of Hosea and Gomer. She has already borne him a son, and now we are going to see them continuing to have kids:

Hosea 1:6 *And she conceived again, and bare a daughter. And God said unto him, Call her name Loruhamah: for I will no more have mercy upon the house of Israel; but I will utterly take them away. 7 But I will have mercy upon the house of Judah, and will save them by the*

221

LORD their God, and will not save them by bow, nor by sword, nor by battle, by horses, nor by horsemen. **8** *Now when she had weaned Loruhamah, she conceived, and bare a son.* **9** *Then said God, Call his name Loammi: for ye are not my people, and I will not be your God.*

What we find thus far is that Hosea has taken Gomer as his wife. This woman was dirty and sinful, and no one would want her for anything other than a one night stand. Yet Hosea has married her. Hosea has loved her. And they have now been together long enough to have three children together. These two have been married for quite a few years now! It had to look to Hosea like they were well on their way and that Gomer had really put her past behind her. But that was not to be.

Hosea 2:1 *Say ye unto your brethren, Ammi; and to your sisters, Ruhamah.* **2** *Plead with your mother, plead: for she is not my wife, neither am I her husband: let her therefore put away her whoredoms out of her sight, and her adulteries from between her breasts;* **3** *Lest I strip her naked, and set her as in the day that she was born, and make her as a wilderness, and set her like a dry land, and slay her with thirst.* **4** *And I will not have mercy upon her children; for they be the children of whoredoms.* **5** *For their mother hath played the harlot: she that conceived them hath done shamefully: for she said, I will go after my lovers, that give me my bread and my water, my wool and my flax, mine oil and my drink.*

After producing at least three children together, the marriage of Hosea and Gomer was shattered. Hosea came home one day, and Gomer was not home.

Hours passed by, perhaps, and Hosea surely must have started getting worried. It should not take her that long to get back from the marketplace. Was she hurt? Had something happened to her?

And then maybe there came a knock on the door. It was the next door neighbor.

"Hosea, I don't know how to tell you this, but I figured you should know. I saw your wife leave out earlier, and she was pulling a suitcase behind her. Hosea, I overheard her. She was talking out loud to herself, and she said, '*I will go after my lovers, that give me my bread and my water, my wool and my flax, mine oil and my drink.*' Hosea, I am real sorry to have to tell you this, I know you love her and all, but it looks like she is gone back to her old ways. Hosea, she is cheating on you, and if I were you I would not expect her to ever come home..."

Oh, my, the devastating hurt and anguish of Hosea! Husbands, can you imagine how you would feel if this was you?

Some of you can imagine it. You, in fact, know exactly how it feels. You have loved someone and treated them right and provided for them, and they have done to you exactly what Gomer did to Hosea. You have gone through the shock, the denial, the hurt, the anger, the bitterness, the whole nine yards.

The question is, what are you going to do?

In some cases, the choice is no longer even yours. She has gone away, broken the marriage, and married someone else. If that is the case, nothing in this passage or in this chapter applies to you or your situation.

But many of you either are now, or at some point in the future will be in the same position as Hosea. A wife has cheated, she is away from home, she is sleeping around, but she has not yet divorced you and married another. And until she does, *The Hosea Option* is still available to you.

What is *The Hosea Option?*

The unbelievable choice of Hosea

Hosea was faced with a choice, and it really was a choice. Based on what she had done, he actually had two ways that he could rightfully go. He could divorce her and move on with his life since she herself had already broken the marriage.

Deuteronomy 24:1 *When a man hath taken a wife, and married her, and it come to pass that she find no favour in his eyes, because he hath found some uncleanness in her: then let him write her a bill of divorcement, and give it in her hand, and send her out of his house.*

This was not the original intent of marriage under God, but under the law it was an option. Christ in the New Testament said the same:

Matthew 19:9 *And I say unto you, Whosoever shall put away his wife, except it be for fornication, and shall marry another, committeth adultery: and whoso marrieth her which is put away doth commit adultery.*

When Jesus said that it was wrong "except it be for fornication," it is abundantly clear that when there was fornication it was not legally wrong!

But it was also not the only option. There was a better option, there was the original option, there was God's way, there was *The Hosea Option.*

You see, God never said a person *had to* divorce a spouse that cheated; He said a person *was allowed* to divorce a spouse that cheated. The fact that something is allowed does not mean that it is desired! There are many things that God allows because of the hardness of men's hearts that God does not desire.

Hosea decided that he would do the unbelievable. Where everyone else in his situation would have thrown away their marriage and never had a single person look down on them, Hosea chose to pursue his straying wife and restore the marriage.

And that, what I call the *Hosea Option*, is the focus of this chapter.

When a spouse strays, husband or wife, and the remaining spouse desires to set things right, what steps are to be followed? Let's look at what Hosea did to find out.

The first thing he did was to maintain the home and the family life without her.

Hosea 2:1 *Say ye unto your brethren, Ammi; and to your sisters, Ruhamah.*

Hosea and all the children were still there. And when she came back, who knows how many months or years later, there was still a happy home to come back to.

When people in these situations come to me, broken, devastated, confused, needing help, I always start them in the same place, and this is it. Maintain the home and family life even without your spouse. A person who has had a spouse leave needs to keep coming to church, and keep reading their Bible, and keep having family night, and keep going on vacation, and keep cutting the grass, and keep washing the car, and keep having cookouts, and keep and keep and keep...

When people have a spouse leave them, they do what comes natural, but what comes natural makes things worse! They go into a depression, and they gain weight, and they let themselves and the house go, and they stop smiling.

And what they have just done is to make themselves that much less of an attractive option to come home to! The enemy, the other man or woman, is smiling and laughing and having a great time with their new toy. And the cheating spouse compares that to what he or she left, and it is no wonder he or she has no desire to come home.

If you are in the situation of Hosea, you are going to have to make yourself do the most unnatural thing imaginable, you are going to have to go on with life and be happy.

You see, Hebrews 11:25 teaches that the pleasure of sin is just for a season. There will come a time, somewhere down the road, when things with the new guy or new girl are no longer fresh and new and pleasant. And when that day comes, that spouse will turn his or her eyes toward home and see how things look back there. And if they see a joyful, happy home, what kind of an effect do you think that will have on his or her heart?

And here is the bonus. If you choose to go on with life and be happy, and yet your spouse never does come back...you are still happy! It is a win for you no matter how the marriage problems end up.

He secondly made it difficult for her to live in her sin.

Hosea 2:6 *Therefore, behold, I will hedge up thy way with thorns, and make a wall, that she shall not find her paths.* **7** *And she shall follow after her lovers, but she shall not overtake them; and she shall seek them, but shall not find them: then shall she say, I will go and return to my first husband; for then was it better with me than now.* **8** *For she did not know that I gave her corn, and wine, and oil, and multiplied her silver and gold, which they prepared for Baal.* **9** *Therefore will I return, and take away my corn in the time thereof, and my wine in the season thereof, and will recover my wool and my flax given to cover her nakedness.* **10** *And now will I discover her lewdness in the sight of her lovers, and none shall deliver her out of mine hand.* **11** *I will also cause all her mirth to cease, her feast days, her new moons, and her sabbaths, and all her solemn feasts.*

Hosea was a very, very wise husband. The second thing he did was he made her life away from home as difficult as he could!

For some reason, this does not seem to occur to people. I have counseled many, many, many people in similar situations, I have spoken to many pastor friends who have as well, and let me tell you some of the true things that we have seen.

A husband who allowed his straying wife to use his car to go pick up her boyfriend, because her car had broken down.

A husband who was having trouble making ends meet because he was still making the car and insurance payments on his straying wife's vehicle.

A wife who had a cheating husband who also would not work, so she worked a ton of extra hours which allowed her husband all the time he needed to go and cheat!

A husband who helped turn the power on at his straying wife's apartment.

A wife who allowed her straying husband to "divide everything evenly, trust me, I'll be fair" instead of getting a lawyer to take him to the cleaners, and she ended up getting taken to the cleaners instead!

If a husband or wife really wants to have a straying spouse come home someday, he or she needs to exercise part two of the Hosea option and make it very difficult for that spouse to live in his or her sin!

Look at what Hosea said he would do:

...I will hedge up thy way with thorns...

...make a wall, that she shall not find her paths...

...take away my corn in the time thereof, and my wine in the season thereof, and will recover my wool and my flax given to cover her nakedness...

...I will also cause all her mirth to cease, her feast days...

That is a pretty tough list! He basically said, "I will make her uncomfortable every step of the way. I will make it hard for her even to get from point A to point B. I will take my groceries from her. I'll even take all the fabric I bought that she was planning on making clothes with. I will make all of her happy days, unhappy days."

Does that sound harsh? It should not. He was trying to get his straying wife to come home! He could have said, "You're filthy and dirty and I hate you and I do not ever want to see you again." That would have been harsh. But making her way in sin difficult to motivate her to come home, that was not harsh, that was the kindest action of all.

If you have a spouse to stray, they should never be able to do so in a vehicle that is in your name, and they should never be given access to your money to do it with, and if they are hungry they need to come and sit at your table to eat.

Put another way, you should never do anything to help someone live in sin!

He thirdly motivated her heart to return.

Hosea 2:14 *Therefore, behold, I will allure her, and bring her into the wilderness, and speak comfortably unto her.* **15** *And I will give her her vineyards from thence, and the valley of Achor for a door of hope: and she shall sing there, as in the days of her youth, and as in the day when she came up out of the land of Egypt.* **16** *And it shall be at that day, saith the LORD, that thou shalt call me Ishi; and shalt call me no more Baali.*

He had already made her life in sin difficult, but when they finally got to speak face to face, she found no harshness at all.

I wonder what this was like. Gomer had been gone, months most likely, and one day either by appointment or by chance, they meet. Maybe it was to speak about one of the children. Whatever it was for, when they met up, Hosea "allured her, brought her into the wilderness, and spoke comfortably to her."

From the moment she walked out, his entire goal was to win her back. And when he saw an opening, he took it. The lover of the moment was obviously not around, and he took the chance to woo her heart. They went away somewhere.

You know, her lovers were only interested in what they could get from her. Hosea took the time to remind her that he was interested in her. What was that like for her, going out into the wilderness with her husband, maybe picking out a great spot overlooking the Dead Sea, taking time to listen to the waves roll in?

She doubtless tried to pick fights, trying to find some reason to hate him. But he just allured her and spoke comfortably to her.

Sir, ma'am, when you are cheated on, everything in you wants to lash out. And if you do, you will feel better for a few minutes...and then not.

But if you can speak alluring, comfortable words...

"Honey, I know what you've done, but I forgive you..."

"Honey, I still think you are pretty..."

"Honey, I sure would love to have you home...

"Honey, we can work all of this out..."

Yes, make his or her life in sin difficult. But not for the purpose of vengeance! Do it for the purpose of getting to part three of the Hosea option, motivating his or her heart to return!

He was also willing to pay the price to bring her back.

Even after their trip into the wilderness, even after alluring and speaking comfortably to her, she still went back to her lovers. But Hosea was not done trying, and one day he heard something:

Hosea 3:1 *Then said the LORD unto me, Go yet, love a woman beloved of her friend, yet an adulteress, according to the love of the LORD toward the children of Israel, who look to other gods, and love flagons of wine. 2 So I bought her to me for fifteen pieces of silver, and for an homer of* *barley, and an half homer of barley:* **3** *And I said unto her, Thou shalt abide for me many days; thou shalt not play the harlot, and thou shalt not be for another man: so will I also be for thee.*

Please allow me to explain what is being spoken of in these verses. One day, word came from the Lord that it was time to go get Gomer. Gomer was at the end of her rope, and today Hosea could bring her home.

What had changed?

Gomer's sin had finally cost her to the point that she was broken. Her lovers had gotten tired of her, and Gomer had been taken to the slave market. There were other, younger, fresher, prettier girls to sleep around with, so her lovers decided they would just get rid of Gomer.

When a person was taken to the slave market, they were stripped naked, and paraded around so that potential buyers could see what they were getting. This is where Gomer's sin had taken her.

The bidding started, and for her, the price was set very low. She was just not worth much to anyone anymore. The bidding had only reached half the price of a female slave in money.

Then she heard a voice bidding, a familiar voice. She no doubt looked up as her heart skipped a beat...and there he was, the preacher, her husband, Hosea. After the way that she wounded him, humiliated him, abandoned him, there he was paying the price for her, not because he needed a slave, but he wanted his wife back.

He was willing to pay the price to get his wife back, and that price was very, very high.

"But preacher, you said the price was very low, just half the price in money of a female slave!"

Not that price. That is not the real price that Hosea paid on that day. Do you know the price he really paid? He had to open up and take out all of his pride...all of his desire for vengeance...all of his hurt...all of his memories of what she had done...and lay them down.

That price paid is what finally won her! That price paid is what finally got her home for good.

Sir, ma'am, if you are going through these fires right now, and if you want your spouse to come home, this is the price you must be willing to pay. But what do you want more? Your pride, your desire for vengeance, your hurt, your memories of what has been done to you? Is that what you really want? Or do you want what Hosea wanted, do you want your spouse back?

By the way, this is what Jesus wanted. He paid the same kind of price for us, His bride! Jesus and Hosea had every right to cast the bride aside forever, but both chose to pay the ultimate price to win their spouse.

Chapter 17
The Couple Who Proved that Togetherness Is Not Always a Good Thing

"Greetings, and please be honest in everything you say on this day.

"I know you think it odd that we begin this letter this way, but when you hear our story, you will understand. In marriage vows, man and woman commonly pledge to love each other till death do them part. My wife and I certainly did. However, I do not imagine that either of us thought our vows would literally end by death from our own lips!

"We were members of the greatest church ever, the church at Jerusalem. And it was in that very church that we died. Not after decades of membership, but after mere days of membership!

"It was our own fault. I died first, right there in church, and then my wife died right there in church just hours later.

"Who are we? Why, we are the couple who proved that togetherness is not always a good thing; we are Ananias and Sapphira!"

Acts 5:1 *But a certain man named Ananias, with Sapphira his wife, sold a possession,* **2** *And kept back part of* *the price, his wife also being privy to it, and brought a certain part, and laid it at the apostles' feet. 3 But Peter said, Ananias, why hath Satan filled thine heart to lie to the Holy Ghost, and to keep back part of the price of the land? 4 Whiles it remained, was it not thine own? and after it was sold, was it not in thine own power? why hast thou conceived this thing in thine heart? thou hast not lied unto men, but unto God. 5 And Ananias hearing these words fell down, and gave up the ghost: and great fear came on all them that heard these things. 6 And the young men arose, wound him up, and carried him out, and buried him. 7 And it was about the space of three hours after, when his wife, not knowing what was done, came in. 8 And Peter answered unto her, Tell me whether ye sold the land for so much? And she said, Yea, for so much. 9 Then Peter said unto her, How is it that ye have agreed together to tempt the Spirit of the Lord? behold, the feet of them which have buried thy husband are at the door, and shall carry thee out. 10 Then fell she down straightway at his feet, and yielded up the ghost: and the young men came in, and found her dead, and, carrying her forth, buried her by her husband. 11 And great fear came upon all the church, and upon as many as heard these things.*

It is hard to imagine a marriage being broken in a more dramatic way than the way this one was broken. God killed the husband, then a few hours later killed the wife! That kind of thing is usually pretty damaging to a marriage. But this was something they brought on themselves, so there will be a lot that we can learn from it in our study on marriage.

The setting

In our text we saw a man and wife both losing their lives for what seems to be such a minor thing. So it would be wise for us to look at the context and find out exactly what was going on.

234

At this time, the early church was just that–early. It was maybe a few weeks or months old! As such, everything that happened was foundational. Everything they did sent a message about what kind of a church they were going to be. This is one of the reasons why God dealt with the sin of Ananias and Sapphira so harshly. Tell me, are you glad people are not being killed for lying today?

But now let's look at exactly why these two did what they did. To see that, we need to go back to the end of chapter four.

Acts 4:34 *Neither was there any among them that lacked: for as many as were possessors of lands or houses sold them, and brought the prices of the things that were sold,* **35** *And laid them down at the apostles' feet: and distribution was made unto every man according as he had need.* **36** *And Joses, who by the apostles was surnamed Barnabas, (which is, being interpreted, The son of consolation,) a Levite, and of the country of Cyprus,* **37** *Having land, sold it, and brought the money, and laid it at the apostles' feet.*

In the early days of the church, you had a situation of great and unexpected need. People had come to Jerusalem by the hundreds of thousands to worship from across the world. A lot of people were saved on the day of Pentecost, and then more and more and more. Those people, who had intended to worship and then leave, stayed!

But they did not have homes or jobs, and that posed a problem. So the members of the early church voluntarily sold a lot of their possessions, and gave that money to the church so that these new Christians could be taken care of.

One man in particular was singled out for attention. A man named Joses sold some land and gave all of the money from it. His character and sacrifice was so great, the apostles called him Barnabbas, the Son of Consolation.

In other words, Barnabbas got famous. And that is what Ananias and Saphira fixated on. They figured he should not be the one getting all of the attention; they should be getting it too.

This is the setting behind what this married couple chose to do that ended up breaking their marriage.

The scheming

Acts 5:1 *But a certain man named Ananias, with Sapphira his wife, sold a possession,* **2** *And kept back part of the price, his wife also being privy to it, and brought a certain part, and laid it at the apostles' feet.*

We need to stipulate right up front that all of this was absolutely unnecessary. To begin with, everything that everyone was doing was voluntary! There was no demand on anyone. This was not socialism; there was no governing body taking everything from people and then divvying it out.

Furthermore, anyone who did sell possessions and give anything was more than welcome to keep as much of it as they liked and give as much of it as they liked. Peter himself said this when confronting Ananias.

Acts 5:4 *Whiles it remained, was it not thine own? and after it was sold, was it not in thine own power?*

What you need to understand is that these two did not die for stealing or even for not giving enough. Can you imagine what it would be like then or even today if people died for not giving? Talk about a way to thin out a church!

These two died for lying. They died for finding a way to get noticed and glorified while lying about what they did to get noticed and glorified. Peter pointed that out also.

Acts 5:4b *...thou hast not lied unto men, but unto God.*

This married couple did wrong, and they planned to do wrong. It was not a spur of the moment thing; it was an intentional decision to do wrong.

The supporting

It is at this point that we will begin to see the real marriage issue. We begin by seeing Ananias come before the church to announce his great deed. His wife was not there at the time.

Acts 5:1 *But a certain man named Ananias, with Sapphira his wife, sold a possession, 2 And kept back part of the price, his wife also being privy to it, and brought a certain part, and laid it at the apostles' feet. 3 But Peter said, Ananias, why hath Satan filled thine heart to lie to the Holy Ghost, and to keep back part of the price of the land? 4 Whiles it remained, was it not thine own? and after it was sold, was it not in thine own power? why hast thou conceived this thing in thine heart? thou hast not lied unto men, but unto God. 5 And Ananias hearing these words fell down, and gave up the ghost: and great fear came on all them that heard these things.*

Ananias came before the apostles, made a grand scene of giving the money, and then listened in horror as Peter busted him in front of everyone. He died right there on the spot.

By the way, there is one thing about the church of Jerusalem that seems amazingly remarkable, apparently everyone there knew how to hold their tongue. Three hours went by, yet in a church with thousands of members, Sapphira somehow did not hear a peep about what had happened!

Well, there was a body lying there on the altar, and something had to be done about that.

Acts 5:6 *And the young men arose, wound him up, and carried him out, and buried him.*

I am betting that is not what they expected when they got up and went to church that day.

It is in the next verse that we get to the heart of the matter.

Acts 5:7 *And it was about the space of three hours after, when his wife, not knowing what was done, came in.* **8** *And Peter answered unto her, Tell me whether ye sold the land for so much? And she said, Yea, for so much.* **9** *Then Peter said unto her,* **How is it that ye have agreed together** *to tempt the Spirit of the Lord? behold, the feet of them which have buried thy husband are at the door, and shall carry thee out.*

That phrase *how is it that ye have agreed together* says it all! Ananias and Sapphira planned ahead of time; Ananias and Sapphira agreed to do wrong.

Whenever wrong is done that two people are involved in, one of them had to think of it first. That means that the other of them supported the first one.

Now, before we deal with that, let me remind you of how it ended.

Acts 5:10 *Then fell she down straightway at his feet, and yielded up the ghost: and the young men came in, and found her dead, and, carrying her forth, buried her by her husband.*

Can we agree that this did not end well?

Can we agree that both of them being dead was, in fact, a negative thing for their marriage?

Can we agree that if they had done right they had the potential to live happily and healthily together for many more good years?

Yes to all of the above! Their "togetherness" in this matter was not a good thing; it was a very bad thing!

If either of them had at any time said, "No, we cannot do this; it is wrong," they would have lived, their marriage would have survived.

If Sapphira, when confronted by Peter, would have said, "No sir, my husband lied," then she would have lived.

Here is the entire point–no one should support his or her spouse in wrongdoing! For their own good, you cannot do it!

I have known of a wife who bought drugs for her husband.

I have known of a wife who knew that her husband was selling drugs, but covered for him at every turn.

I have known a husband whose wife threw temper tantrum after temper tantrum, and he backed her up even when he knew she was dead wrong.

I knew a husband whose wife lied, constantly, and he backed up whatever she said.

Some of you are probably sitting here a bit uncomfortable and maybe thinking, "But I want my spouse to back me up no matter what!" You better heed the words of Scripture.

Proverbs 27:6 *Faithful are the wounds of a friend; but the kisses of an enemy are deceitful.*

It is a friend that is willing to wound you when you need it. Only an enemy puckers up and kisses you when you need to be rebuked. I want my wife to be a friend enough to me to keep me out of trouble by telling me when I am wrong!

Men are the world's worst at expecting their wives to back them up no matter what. And many of them teach their wives to do so. But if Sapphira had had enough character to say to her husband, "No, we are not going to do this; it is wrong," he would not have died on the altar.

Sir, if your wife is wrong on something, you do not need to support her in that wrong; you need to tell her she is wrong.

Ma'am, if your husband is wrong on something, you do not need to support him in that wrong; you need to tell him he is wrong.

"I don't agree with you, you heretical preacher; a wife needs to support her husband no matter what!"

Um, "He" disagrees.

He who?

He, God.

Acts 5:9 *Then Peter said unto her, How is it that ye have agreed together to tempt the Spirit of the Lord? behold, the feet of them which have buried thy husband are at the door, and shall carry thee out. 10 Then fell she down straightway at his feet, and yielded up the ghost: and the young men came in, and found her dead, and, carrying her forth, buried her by her husband.*

If God had agreed with what she did, she would not have died on the altar. God did not praise her for supporting her husband in his wrong; He killed her for it! Do you not think that is fairly conclusive proof that He did not approve of her supporting Ananias in his wrong?

Some years ago we had a wife show up at our church who really made a big deal over the wife's "responsibility to always obey and follow her husband, no matter what." It was very clearly the biggest issue in the world to her. She would bring it up every single week, even when no one else was talking about it in any way!

Have you ever just gotten a really creepy feeling about something or someone? I got one.

So we did a little investigating. Turns out this woman was married to a man who liked children. I mean he really LIKED children.

So you tell me, parents, would you rather she support her husband in his wrong, or would you rather she confront her husband in his wrong?

There is exactly one person who is always right and always pure, and that is God. He does not need anyone confronting Him, but all of the rest of us do!

Ma'am, if you want your marriage to survive and thrive, then you do not ever need to support your husband when he does wrong; you need to be the one to confront him over it.

Sir, if you want your marriage to survive and thrive, then you do not ever need to support your wife when she does wrong; you need to be the one to confront her over it.

If you ever forget that, or if you are ever unsure about it, go view the side by side grave stones of Ananias and Sapphira. His says "Agreed together" and hers says "To tempt the Lord."

Chapter 18
The Greatest Husband of All Times

"Hello, My bride, as always, you are the fairest of the fair to Me. How long has it been now since I first laid eyes on you? There literally are no number of years I can give for an answer, for My eyes have been upon you from eternity past.

"Many have imagined their bride to be spotless, but you, My bride, truly are! I see in you no spot, no blemish, no flaw, nothing to make Me ever want to divert My gaze from you.

"Does that surprise you? I know that you know your sins and flaws and failings. But, My bride, to Me you are altogether lovely, for I Myself have put away every single one of your impurities.

"My bride, you have grown up hearing fairy tales that end with the words 'and they lived happily ever after.' Those words, dear bride, have never been true. But they will be, one day, for you and Me. I promised to come back for you, and receive you unto Myself, that where I am ye shall be also, and I will. You and I, My dear bride, will then truly live happily ever after! The mansion is finished, the supper is prepared, and I am simply waiting for My Father to give the word.

"Be listening for the trumpet, My bride, and be ready each and every day to leave. Until then, I remain yours.

"Jesus."

We have covered chapter after chapter and marriage after marriage. We have seen good husbands and bad husbands, good wives and bad wives. But we have never, ever seen a perfect husband.

That will change right here and right now. We have saved the very best for last. If you want to know how to be a marriage maker, if you want to know how to be the perfect husband, all you have to do is be like Christ and you will accomplish that goal! You see, Jesus described Himself in terms of being a bridegroom, a husband, and He described us in terms of being a bride, a wife! So if we find out how He treats His spouse, then we will obviously know how to treat ours.

Matthew 25:1 *Then shall the kingdom of heaven be likened unto ten virgins, which took their lamps, and went forth to meet the bridegroom. 2 And five of them were wise, and five were foolish. 3 They that were foolish took their lamps, and took no oil with them: 4 But the wise took oil in their vessels with their lamps. 5 While the bridegroom tarried, they all slumbered and slept. 6 And at midnight there was a cry made, Behold, the bridegroom cometh; go ye out to meet him. 7 Then all those virgins arose, and trimmed their lamps. 8 And the foolish said unto the wise, Give us of your oil; for our lamps are gone out. 9 But the wise answered, saying, Not so; lest there be not enough for us and you: but go ye rather to them that sell, and buy for yourselves. 10 And while they went to buy, the bridegroom came; and they that were ready went in with him to the marriage: and the door was shut. 11 Afterward came also the other virgins, saying, Lord, Lord, open to us. 12 But he answered and said, Verily I say unto you, I know you not. 13*

Watch therefore, for ye know neither the day nor the hour wherein the Son of man cometh.

It is clear from this passage that Jesus is likening Himself to a bridegroom, a husband. He uses the term bridegroom in verses one, five, six, and ten, then He refers it to Himself in verse thirteen when He calls the bridegroom the "Son of man." That is His favorite title for Himself in the gospels.

This is not the only place we find this concept. One of the more famous one is in Ephesians 5.

Ephesians 5:23 *For the husband is the head of the wife, even as Christ is the head of the church: and he is the saviour of the body.* **24** *Therefore as the church is subject unto Christ, so let the wives be to their own husbands in every thing.* **25** *Husbands, love your wives, even as Christ also loved the church, and gave himself for it;* **26** *That he might sanctify and cleanse it with the washing of water by the word,* **27** *That he might present it to himself a glorious church, not having spot, or wrinkle, or any such thing; but that it should be holy and without blemish.* **28** *So ought men to love their wives as their own bodies. He that loveth his wife loveth himself.* **29** *For no man ever yet hated his own flesh; but nourisheth and cherisheth it, even as the Lord the church:* **30** *For we are members of his body, of his flesh, and of his bones.* **31** *For this cause shall a man leave his father and mother, and shall be joined unto his wife, and they two shall be one flesh.* **32** *This is a great mystery: but I speak concerning Christ and the church.*

Over and over in these verses Paul bounces back and forth from the relationship of husband and wife to the relationship between Christ and the church.

Here is another one:

Revelation 21:9 *And there came unto me one of the seven angels which had the seven vials full of the seven last plagues, and talked with me, saying, Come hither, I will* *shew thee the bride, the Lamb's wife.* **10** *And he carried me away in the spirit to a great and high mountain, and shewed me that great city, the holy Jerusalem, descending out of heaven from God,*

Here we specifically see the phrase *the bride, the Lamb's wife.* By the way, please do not think that the city is the Lamb's wife, that is ridiculous, it is the people within the city that make up the Lamb's wife, it is the saved, it is the church!

When you see in the Garden of Eden that the very first relationship God put together was a man and wife, it is evident that this relationship is very essential to Him. Our man and wife marriage is simply a picture of His marriage to us.

And that brings us again to our study of marriage.

Can we agree that Christ is perfect in all that he does? Yes, of course. In that case, finding out how He treats His spouse will tell us husbands especially how we ought to treat our wives.

Clearly, there is no way we could ever cover all that He does or does not do in one chapter, but we will at least deal with some of the main things.

Jesus took the lead, but all for our benefit, not for His own

Ephesians 5:23 *For the husband is the head of the wife, even as Christ is the head of the church: and he is the saviour of the body.*

Ephesians 5 has become one of the most hated passages in the entire Bible in our "modern, enlightened day." There are two primary reasons for that.

One, wicked women hate the order that God Himself set up.

Two, wicked men under the guise of religion have abused the order that God set up and have warped it so badly as to make it unrecognizable!

The first thing that God began to teach about His husbandly view of marriage is that the man is the head of the home. But how many times have you heard this verse quoted in its entirety?

Rarely.

Here is how you are going to hear this verse quoted probably 99% of the time.

Ephesians 5:23 *For the husband is the head of the wife, even as Christ is the head of the church.* (Period).

But there is no period there. The sentence is not over yet. The whole sentence and the whole verse reads:

Ephesians 5:23 *For the husband is the head of the wife, even as Christ is the head of the church:* ***and he is the saviour of the body.***

Sir, the headship of Christ was for our benefit, not for His own! And your headship in your relationship with your wife is for her benefit, not your own! Any husband who lords his headship over his wife, belittling her and shouting at her and making her feel like a doormat is not following the model of Christ!

His headship resulted in us being saved and in Him being crucified.

His headship resulted in Him becoming dirty with our sin and in us becoming clean with His righteousness.

His headship resulted in us becoming children of the Father while He was crying out to His Father, *"My God, my God, why hast thou forsaken me?"*

His headship resulted in Him ending up on earth so that we could end up in heaven.

His headship resulted in Him dying so that we could live.

247

His headship resulted in Him being punished so that we would not have to.

Every ounce of the headship of Christ was used in such a way as to benefit us at a great cost to Himself!

Sir, be the head of your home. But be the kind of head that Christ was! The very moment you use that headship in such a way to benefit yourself and cost your wife, you have ceased to be the kind of husband that Jesus is to His bride.

Jesus loved His bride, and His every loving effort produced a far better bride

Ephesians 5:25 *Husbands, love your wives, even as Christ also loved the church, and gave himself for it;* **26** *That he might sanctify and cleanse it with the washing of water by the word,* **27** *That he might present it to himself a glorious church, not having spot, or wrinkle, or any such thing; but that it should be holy and without blemish.*

When men get to Ephesians 5, it seems they invariably gravitate toward verse twenty-two before, and maybe even to the exclusion of all others:

Ephesians 5:22 *Wives, submit yourselves unto your own husbands, as unto the Lord.*

I often wonder why they do not start at verse eighteen:

Ephesians 5:18 *And be not drunk with wine, wherein is excess;* ***but be filled with the Spirit;***

Focusing on and obeying that command to be filled with the Spirit would change most everything for the better!

But if not verse eighteen, why not start at verse twenty-one:

Ephesians 5:21 *Submitting yourselves one to another in the fear of God.*

Before God ever told the wife to submit to the husband, He told them both to submit to each other. That sounds kind of important, don't you think?

But if not verse eighteen or verse twenty-one, why not start at verse twenty-five?

Ephesians 5:25 *Husbands, love your wives, even as Christ also loved the church, and gave himself for it;*

In all of my years of pastoring and counseling, I have very rarely ever seen a woman have trouble submitting to a man who truly loved her like Christ loved the church!

How good of a husband is Jesus to His bride? This verse tells us that He loved it and gave Himself for it. Acts 20:28 tells us that He purchased it with His own blood.

Was the bride worthy of all that? Is it that you and I were so sweet, so pure, so consistent, so holy, that He just did not have any choice but to love us like that? You know better than that. **Romans 5:8** says *But God commendeth his love toward us, in that, while we were yet sinners, Christ died for us.*

Jesus, the husband, loved His wife, the church, enough to die for her when she was filthy and stubborn and wicked and hateful and lost! He paid the ultimate price for a bride who had no worthiness in herself!

And what was the result of that love? Look at the rest of the sentence, which is found in verses twenty-six and twenty-seven.

Ephesians 5:26 *That he might sanctify and cleanse it with the washing of water by the word,* **27** *That he might present it to himself a glorious church, not having spot, or wrinkle, or any such thing; but that it should be holy and without blemish.*

He loved us and gave Himself for us so that we could become glorious and holy with no spots and no wrinkles and no blemishes. His love produced in His bride what harshness and anger and demands never could!

May I tell you who, or what, rather, was harsh and angry and demanding? It was called the law. For thousands of years humanity was under the law. For thousands of years it was one demand after another, and no matter how hard anyone ever tried it was never good enough, and it never made anyone any better.

So what was the purpose of that?

Galatians 3:24 *Wherefore the law was our schoolmaster to bring us unto Christ, that we might be justified by faith.*

The law was designed to make us realize that we could not possibly be good enough by our efforts; the law was designed to make us finally break under the pressure and turn to Christ for help!

Basically, in the context of marriage, the law was designed to show us how a cruel, harsh, demanding spouse would be, so that we could seek out the loving arms of Jesus.

But, men, do you understand the picture this paints for you in your marriage? You have one of two choices, you have one of two patterns that you can choose to follow. You can either choose to be a husband patterned after the law: harsh, stern, demanding, overbearing; or you can choose to be a husband patterned after Jesus, who was loving and giving and kind.

You also have one of two results that will come from the choice that you make.

If you choose to be a husband patterned after the law, you will most likely have the same results as the law had. You will produce an outward conformity but inward resentment in your spouse, and there will be no real love at all. She will fear you and maybe even respect you, but will not likely truly ever love you. In other words, your demands and harshness will not really produce a good wife!

But if you choose to be a husband patterned after Christ, you will most likely have the same results that He had. You will likely produce a wife that responds to your love and sacrifice and becomes a glorious, loving, devoted wife!

I have been around marriages for a very long time now, and I have seen a lot. I believe with all my heart I have a wife that loves and adores me. She is fun to be around, she fulfills my desires, she brightens up my day, and I believe it is because I have patterned my husbandry as best as I can after Christ.

I have seen the effects of the "law patterned" husband, especially among people in Bible colleges. I do not remember it ever going too well. I do remember seeing a lot of homes break up, and a lot of would-be preachers going back to hanging drywall or driving a truck. I do remember seeing even the homes that survived produce wives that were just hollow shells, who very rarely smiled, and looked like they were prisoners of war.

Sir, if that is what you are after, you are a sick little man. I want my wife to have fire in her eyes. I want her to have a thousand watt smile that lights up a room. I want her to know that she is beautiful and that I know that she beautiful, and that I know that she knows she is beautiful. I want to love her so well that I am able to present her to myself day after day after day for the rest of our lives as a glorious wife!

Jesus nourished and cherished His bride

Ephesians 5:29 *For no man ever yet hated his own flesh; but **nourisheth** and **cherisheth** it, even as the Lord the church:*

These two words are significant in the context of marriage.

When we read that Jesus nourishes His bride, it is a word that paints the picture of tenderly leading and feeding someone with the purpose of helping them to grow. It is the exact opposite of impatience and badgering.

I meet a great many men who want their wives to be better at this and more efficient at that and more mature about the other, but they have no clue how to get them there. The methodology that the Lord uses with His bride is to nourish, to tenderly lead and feed someone with the purpose of helping them to grow. The methodology that many men use is to raise their voice and hurl insults and make her feel bad enough that she will do better.

A man who does that is a very unskilled husband. The only marriage tool he knows how to handle is a sledge hammer, but a sledgehammer breaks a precious vase.

Years ago I was privileged to tour the Fenton Glass Company, where they handmade some of the most precious and sought after glassware on the planet. There was no one using a hammer on those pieces anywhere! Everything was done gingerly and carefully, and the result was precious and often near priceless.

Sir, you do not need to treat your wife like a two by four to be cut and hammered, you need to treat her like fine china to be formed and fashioned with love and care. When we read that Jesus cherishes His bride, it is the picture of someone on a cold day wrapping someone up to keep them safe and warm and hugging them tightly to Himself.

Men, this world can be a cold and hard place to our wives. But there ought to be one place that they can count on to never be cold and hard, and that is in our presence. In our presence they ought to feel safe and warm and cared for. We ought to be able to make the cares of the world fall away from them when they are in our presence.

You say, "Preacher! That stuff sounds sissified! I'm a real man; I don't do that 'touchy/feely' stuff."

Excuse me? Did you just call Jesus a sissy? Because He is the one described here as nourishing and cherishing

His bride. He was man enough to get beaten to ribbons and still carry a cross up to Calvary; I do not think even as a man that you would have wanted to tangle with Him.

Sir, it is not the overbearing ogre of a husband that is demonstrating manhood; all he is demonstrating is that he is a little girlie man who is so insecure and inferior that he has to take his frustrations out on a woman. That kind of a man you might not want to raise your voice to, because he may cry and wet himself.

It is the man who can tenderly nourish and cherish a wife that is demonstrating real manhood, just like Jesus!

For Jesus, marriage was a "one flesh" kind of thing

Ephesians 5:31 *For this cause shall a man leave his father and mother, and shall be joined unto his wife, and they two shall be one flesh. 32 This is a great mystery: but I speak concerning Christ and the church.*

Way back in the Garden of Eden, we first find the phrase "one flesh."

Genesis 2:24 *Therefore shall a man leave his father and his mother, and shall cleave unto his wife: and they shall be one flesh.*

It should not be surprising that it was in the context of marriage! For 4,000 or more years people used that phrase "one flesh, one flesh, one flesh" to describe the relationship of husband and wife. And then after 4,000 or more years Paul said, "Oh, by the way, that one flesh thing? It is about human marriage, yes, but what it is REALLY about is Christ's relationship with us!"

In other words, when Jesus went into this relationship with us, as far as He was concerned there was no going back, no reservations, it was forever, under any and all circumstances. That attitude is the exact same attitude we are to approach marriage with, and it is to start with the husband! Sir, did Jesus quit on you? No, but He certainly did have plenty of reasons to! But He always set each and every one of those aside and kept right on at it.

There was no Plan B for the Lord in His relationship with us. There is not to be a Plan B in a man's relationships with his wife either.

We have been through eighteen chapters, covering marriage from just about every conceivable angle. Through God's Word you now have the tools to make it work.

Make it work!

In fact, you now have the tools to make it heaven on earth. So make it heaven on earth, marriage maker, make it heaven on earth!

Sources

Robert Jamieson, A. R. Fausset, David Brown, *A Commentary on the Old and New Testaments*

Matthew Henry, *Commentary on the Whole Bible*

James Burton Cofman, *Coffman Commentary on Esther*

Other books by Dr. Bo Wagner

From Footers to Finish Nails

Beyond the Colored Coat

Nehemiah: A Labor of Love

Esther: Five Feasts and the Finger Prints of God

Daniel: Breathtaking

Don't Muzzle the Ox

I'm Saved! Now What???

Fiction Books

The Night Heroes: A Cry from the Coal Mine

The Night Heroes: Free Fall

The Night Heroes: Broken Brotherhood

The Night Heroes: The Blade of Black Crow

Made in United States
North Haven, CT
05 November 2021

10879031R00144